Postcards from Palm Springs

By Robert Julian

ISBN 978-1-4303-2284-9

Individual copies of this book may be purchased online at
www.lulu.com

Wholesale distribution to booksellers and retailers is provided by
Ingram Publishing Services
www.ingrambook.com

Media inquiries and interview requests should be directed to:
postcardsfromps@aol.com

Cover Design by PMA Associates

Library of Congress Cataloging-in-Publication Data

Julian, Robert.
        Postcards from Palm Springs / by Robert Julian.
        1. Julian, Robert. 2. Palm Springs (Palm Springs, California)-
Social life and customs. 3. Writers-United States-Biography. 4. Motion
Picture Industry-United States. I. Title

Acknowledgements

Yes, you can skip this part. I can't. And I wouldn't want to, even if I could. Acknowledgements are like Oscar speeches where the winner makes an ass of himself giving thanks to people unknown to his audience. Here I go. Try to imagine me in a tuxedo, tear-stained and borderline incoherent, babbling wildly behind a podium.

The talented Scott Brassart helped me shape and refine this book with his expert editorial assistance and, more importantly, he convinced me it was worth completing. Earl Greenburg and Don Spradlin, thank you for gifting me with your time and for tolerating me. Rufus Battles, sweetheart, oh…you know. For excellent book design and ongoing support, I thank PMA Associates for rendering services above and beyond the call of booty. Special thanks to my editor at the *Bay Area Reporter*, Roberto Friedman, and to publisher Tom Horn whose newspaper has published my work regularly for the last sixteen years.

Many names in this book were changed to protect the privacy of certain individuals. And although I have good recall, and even better notes, some conversations were reconstructed from memory. If they vary somewhat from the recollection of others who were present, I accept sole responsibility for the way they are expressed on these pages.

Excerpts from Chapters One and Six of this book were serialized by the *Bay Area Reporter* in four installments under the title "My Life on the Z List," appearing in the May 10, May 17, May 24, and May 31, 2007 issues of the paper. Chapter Eight, "Ten Cents a Prance," appeared in abbreviated form in the April 12, 2007 issue of the *Bay Area Reporter* under the same title. Portions of my Earl

Greenburg interview also appeared in the *Bay Area Reporter* on January 4, 2007 under the title "Leader of the Pack."

Now imagine me wiping flop sweat from my brow and speed talking. The conductor brings up the music but I refuse to surrender the podium because I have one last, wildly improbable shout-out in me.

I want to thank the black drag queens who performed in Detroit gay bars like Morey's and Bookie's in the early 1970s. These men were black when it wasn't popular and gay when it wasn't acceptable. Yet they faced the world, sometimes in full makeup and chiffon, without hesitation or reservation. Their unflinching determination to be who they were in the face of incredible obstacles continues to inspire me now as it did so many years ago.

Prologue

Thirty-one years of my life are now dispatched, discarded, or donated - without receipt requested - to the only non-profit that agrees to arrive immediately after the moving van pulls away from the curb. All that remains is the microwave, my large-screen plasma television, and Little Bill, who prances nervously around the empty apartment fretting over his missing toys, his departed water bowl, and the favored mohair throw that no longer drapes over the corner of my absent sofa. Lhasa Apsos are temple dogs who become needy and insecure when their domain is desecrated. Beneath the shadow of his white bangs, Bill's big brown eyes look up and ask, "Are you leaving me behind?"

"Oh, Bill," I sigh. My response echoes in emptiness. I sit on the floor and lean back against the glass wall of the living room that overlooks the street. Bill climbs onto my lap and curls into place, resting his chin on my knee.

"As if I could ever leave you," I murmur in reassurance.

I am fifty-five years old. Fifty-five is the age at which civil servants retire with a nice, steady pension and fully paid health insurance. It's the age at which successful heterosexual men are hitting their stride in their respective professions, cuddling grandchildren, and booking vacations with a second or third wife to some exotic foreign locale. But for a gay man, it is well past the age of invisibility. Fifty-five in the gay world is the equivalent of seventy-five in the straight world. A gay man with a driver's license establishing such a wizened state of decrepitude will not merit a sideways glance from any young hottie unless the geezer in question is famous, driving a Bentley coupe, or has blank checks dangling from the empire waistline of his Sansabelt slacks.

A gay man in his fifties is simply a dinosaur. There is no place in the au courant world of gay bars, discos, and circuit parties for men past the half-century mark. Yet I am wiping the slate clean and starting over in a new city, abandoning my six-figure income as a real estate broker and a practice carefully built over thirteen years for the opportunity of reinventing myself in a new place. I am saying goodbye to one profession and thirty-one years of San Francisco life and heading south to Palm Springs.

I have no intention of abandoning journalism. But articles about film, television, and books, published in the alternative press, are like forgotten pinwheel mints that languish in the bottom of discarded handbags. My earnings as a writer are consistently less than $3,000 a year. Yet the mortgage payment, health insurance premiums, property taxes and other assorted bills continue to crowd my mailbox.

I hear Tony's footfalls on the twenty-nine stairs leading to the front door of my apartment. He pushes open the door without knocking and Bill runs toward the familiar scent of his frequent dog-sitter.

"Come on," Tony insists as he stoops to pet Bill, "let's get this show on the road. I had a shitty day at work and I'm dead tired." He is his usual, cranky, impatient, Virgo self, none too pleased at having his usual routine interrupted

With few words, we march up and down the twenty-nine steps, loading an unneeded microwave into his truck and maneuvering the heavy television into the back seat of my car – the latter inconvenience necessitated by the moving company's adamant refusal to transport a plasma TV screen.

It is dusk. The streetlights on Clifford Terrace spring to life as light rain blows in from the ocean, floating over the treetops of Golden Gate Park and descending on the western slope of Ashbury Heights. Bill stands on his hind legs in the passenger seat of my car with front paws braced against the door and nose pressed to the window. Now convinced he will be part of the upcoming journey, he wags his tail and stares at the two men standing in the rain on the sidewalk.

"Well, I guess this is it," Tony shrugs. He gives me a hug and I pull him close.

"Yeah, I guess it is."

I hold him tight, sensing his discomfort as we both fall victim to the spontaneous onset of lockjaw, an affliction that strikes most men in emotional moments. There will be no goodbyes. Three decades of shared experience in San Francisco have already brought too many of those.

Tony breaks from my embrace and sprints toward his truck.

I call after him, "Think of me when you nuke a cup of coffee."

Without looking back, he shouts, "Have a safe trip."

An hour later, Little Bill sits curled in the passenger seat of my car, oblivious to the heavy rain assaulting the windshield. The storm intensifies as we trudge down Highway 5, the central freeway connecting Northern and Southern California. According to weather forecasts, the Napa and Russian Rivers north of San Francisco will soon overflow their banks. After several days of winter rains, hillside homes are abandoning their foundations, reconfiguring themselves into parallelograms of muddy bewilderment that slouch just beyond futile strands of yellow police tape.

The migration of gay people to Palm Springs in the last five years continues to transform life in the small city once known as the "playground of the stars." It is as if someone shook the tree of Northern California and all the fruit rolled south into the Coachella Valley. Forty percent of the current adult population of Palm Springs is now estimated to be gay or lesbian.

The rain lightens as we approach Harris Ranch and although I cannot see the stockyards in the darkness that surrounds me, the smell of manure creeps into the car. Speeding toward the grapevine and Los Angeles I pop a CD it into the stereo, depending on the blaring R&B soundtrack to keep me awake as the journey lengthens. I am dry-eyed and resolute. I leave San Francisco with no regrets and no unfinished business.

The audible sound coming from the car speakers is vintage Aretha Franklin, recorded live in Paris at the Olympia Theater in 1968. But my voyage has its own mantra. Wheels spin beneath an engine that hums to an asphalt vibration: *let's go let's go.*

-1-

Hidden Palms

Even over the telephone you can tell Carol Grant of Carol Grant Casting doesn't work by the hour. "They want to call the series 'Palm Springs' but it looks like someone owns the title," she explains with rat-a-tat-tat precision. "Anyway, we need shoppers. We're shooting on Palm Canyon Drive and the call is for 4 p.m. You should get about three hours work. Some people will be asked to stay for scenes in the coffee shop after."

Three hours work as an extra on what is known as "The Untitled Kevin Williamson Project" sounds perfect.

"Okay. That works for me. How should I dress?"

"Dress as you would for shopping. There is work available Tuesday night as well. That one is a cocktail party and dinner at a country club. It's shooting at Parker and you need to wear something you would wear to a country club, but not too dressy. That shoot will start late and run into the morning. You'd have to be willing to work all night."

"That's okay."

"Now for tomorrow we need all kinds of shoppers. On the application there was a question about 'would you play gay.'"

Now we're getting down to it. I cut to the chase.

"I *am* gay. I wouldn't have a problem with that."

"Great. Just follow the signs and park in the lot behind Desert Fashion Plaza. There will be people to direct you to check-in. Don't forget to bring a second choice of wardrobe and make sure it's upscale."

I don't need the big yellow "UKWP" signs to find Hollywood in downtown Palm Springs. The shiny white 18-wheelers parked on the street indicate glamour on Goodyear is in town for a location shoot. I follow the signs to the parking lot and the large white tent. Inside, extras mingle, standing or sitting on folding chairs beside long rows of tables. Around the periphery craft services has set up steam tables, a salad bar, and coolers with iced tea and lemonade. I get in a line with other extras to pick up the releases, payment voucher, and IRS forms, checking-in with Jill who finds my name on a long list under the heading "Gay male shoppers." There is one other name below mine; a new boyfriend is in the offing.

Chaos rules. This is an outdoor shoot and the desert's typically mild weather has turned threatening. It is warm and humid inside the tent and dark, ominous gray clouds laden with moisture hover over the San Jacinto Mountains. Deserted Palm Canyon Drive, closed for the evening, now needs parked cars.

A skinny male production assistant shouts, "Is there anyone here with a parked car who can move it to the street for us? We need cars on the street," he pleads, like a carnival barker shilling for quarters. A cord dangles from his earpiece and he talks into a hand-held device as he escorts volunteers out to move their cars. Other extras, cast to drive their cars up and down the street during the shoot, are led off to wardrobe.

Assembled beneath the tent are two hunky black rappers, a host of middle-aged Caucasians, and a gaggle of Red Hat ladies who all wear purple dresses. One woman stands out because she looks as if she has been preserved in mothballs for 50 years. Resting on her aluminum walker, she speaks with a Southern accent and wears a teal wool suit, accented by a ratty mink stole and hat. At least 75 years old, this woman could have been flown in directly from Sunday morning church services at Petticoat Junction. Most surprisingly, she is absolutely real - not a creation of the wardrobe and casting departments. This is who she is.

With no provocation, a short woman in a linen pantsuit suit marches over to my side.

"This shit don't work for me," she insinuates. "I took off work all day today, 'cause they told me to be here at 7 a.m. Then they called and said to come at 4 p.m. And they want me for only three hours? I was in *Sister Act*, you know. With Whoopi. I look a bit like her."

Actually she looks like a Ninja turtle, but I have to ask, "*Sister Act* one, or *Sister Act II*?"

"The first one."

"That was filmed in San Francisco," I remind her.

"That's where I'm from."

"Me, too."

Uninterested in anything that does not emerge from her own mouth, she ignores any inference of camaraderie.

"They don't have their shit together. This is just a damn pilot. If I'd known that I wouldn't have even bothered. This ain't like a Hollywood movie. On a Hollywood movie everyone is in place and ready the moment they supposed to be."

She glances left and spots the banquet tables.

"Oh. They got food," she announces as she beelines for the paper plates and plastic utensils.

A bedraggled production assistant in tank top and beige jeans stands up and pushes herself away from one of the long folding tables. I've been watching her compulsively stroking her brown, *That Girl* bob, as if flattening out that flip of hair might calm her nerves.

"All my shoppers who are checked-in, follow me to wardrobe."

Twenty of us follow her over to the white trucks. The first truck is the wardrobe trailer, where two women and one remarkably sanguine, apparently gay man size-up each extra for the look they want. The male costumer has shoulder-length brown hair and too much stomach, but he bears the unflappable air of one who has seen and done it all. I'm sure he was quite a knockout twenty years ago. Even now I'm drawn to his low-key approach and gentle demeanor.

"And who are you supposed to be?" he inquires matter-of-factly, with none of that looking-down-over-eyeglasses condescension.

"A gay shopper" I reply, in my khakis and crew-necked t-shirt. I feel like a second grader who has just turned in his penmanship exercise and awaits the approval of his teacher.

The costumer fixates on my shoes, a lime green pair of deck shoes I picked up on a lark at the outlet mall.

"What do you have in that bag?"

"A pair of Diesel jeans and a turquoise shirt."

"Unless you have a pair of shorts I'm going to put you in something else."

"I don't."

He disappears into the wardrobe trailer and emerges with lime green plaid shorts and a polo shirt that precisely match my shoes.

"These are vintage," he explains. "Go try them on and let us take a look."

The next 18-wheeler resting curbside is configured as four separate dressing rooms. I climb the short metal staircase and enter one of the rooms to change. The shorts and shirt fit perfectly. Returning to the costumer, I'm given an enthusiastic seal of approval and an introduction to my new boyfriend.

Matthew is 28 and a vision in powder blue. Standing beside each other, we look like a couple of gay psychedelic ice cream cones. We are a May/December couple, something easy for Matthew to accept since his current Palm Springs lover is a retired dentist, 32 years his senior.

With arms around each other's waists, the newly conjoined gay shoppers head for the set: a two-block stretch of Palm Canyon that begins with the abominable life-sized bronze statue of Sonny Bono and continues past

Enzo's restaurant where the coffee shop scene will be shot.

An assistant director places us on the sidewalk and gives us our directions. She asks, "Now what are you supposed to be?"

"Gay shoppers," we reply.

"Okay. Well, when the director calls 'action' do whatever it is you do. What do you do, anyway?"

Without missing a beat, I reply, "Fellatio."

She laughs so hard she has to ask the director to repeat the instruction coming in over her earpiece. For the rest of the evening, whenever I catch her eye I mouth the word "fellatio." It cracks her up every time.

On the set, extras are not called extras; they are "background." And stand-ins are called the "second team." The stars are the "first team;" they replace the "second team" after lighting and camera angles are set. Tonight one of them is Taylor Handley, formerly of *The O.C.*, who is 21 but plays a mop-topped addict of 16. His love interest is Amber Heard, a teen siren out of the Medusa cum Brigitte Bardot mold currently inspiring erections among the skateboard set.

Williamson's proposed television series involves a young boy (Handley) with a substance abuse problem whose mother (Gayle O'Grady from *American Dreams*) moves him to a gated Palm Springs community, equating suburban relocation with rehab. Handley's character rides a bicycle this evening to meet Heard's character at the coffee shop that was, until a few hours ago, Enzo's Italian restaurant.

Twenty cars and drivers move back and forth as the establishing street shot is executed more times than any of the extras can remember. Each time, the cars must back up and begin again from precisely the same spot, maintaining their original position and distance from each other. All the extras must also move in the same way, at the same speed, for multiple takes. This continues for almost four hours. Cameras, lights, cords, microphones, and reflectors insinuate themselves into corners and sidewalks just beyond view of the camera lens. Considering the tedium involved, the cast and crew are remarkably patient and good-natured.

When lunch is called, everyone heads back to the tent for dinner. On the way, my new boyfriend, Matthew, tells me he met his lover over the Internet. "I weighed 240 pounds in high school," he volunteers, "and I didn't get circumcised until I was 23 years old."

Why, I wonder, do people tell me these things?

After lunch, the good will of the evening wears thin as the proposed three-hour shoot runs into the frigid night. The crew passes out bottled water to help the background players avoid dehydration. We can't carry them while filming so we park them behind trees, plants and benches, making sure they are far enough away to be out of the shot. With the cameras rolling, we watch helplessly as a homeless man with a shopping cart deftly pushes his chariot along the sidewalk, absconding with all our carefully stashed imminently recyclable bottles of water.

As extras, we are both expendable and necessary. Extras provide movement, context, and a sense of reality the production would not have without them. When we are given a sidewalk placement and specific movement for a scene we are expected to remember it and repeat it until the director is satisfied he has what he needs on film. Each time we re-shoot, the background players and automobiles are instructed to reset.

At the end of a take, the assistant director corrals all within earshot and calls out, "Background, reset to one." This is followed by, "camera is rolling" and then "action," which is our cue to move. These three directives, which always follow in sequence, are the extra's theme song.

I walk the streets of Palm Canyon all night, getting blistered feet and frayed nerves in what ultimately

16

becomes a literal forced march. I have stepped on Ruby
Keeler's and William Powell's stars on the Palm Canyon
Walk of Stars so often, I imagine them rising from their
graves and asking a production assistant to bitch-slap me
for my insolence. My pay: $54 for eight hours, plus time-
and-a-half for overtime. Tonight's proposed three-hour
shoot lasts 10 hours and 45 minutes.

Sometime after midnight and before we are
released to go home, my newly assigned boyfriend,
Matthew, points out a guy standing quietly alone in the
shadows of a doorway near the Plaza Theater, about 50
yards from the camera.

"Look," he whispers, "it's Kevin Williamson."

Auteur of the untitled, Williamson seems deeply
absorbed in thought about something, or someone, a
million miles away. He is as much absent as present. There
is a lot riding on this production – money, careers, and
industry clout. And at this point, it's a crap shoot.
Williamson is one of the few openly gay writer/producers
working on this level in Hollywood; his *Dawson's Creek* was
a phenomenon. But what if no one picks up the new
series?

At 3 a.m., I turn in my time sheet, lining up behind
the Whoopi manqué who has stayed to the bitterly cold
end, and I stagger to my car. The next shoot begins in

thirteen hours. I'll play an upscale country club member and I've been forewarned we'll be shooting all night at Parker. I haven't pulled two consecutive all-nighters in a row since my Organic Chemistry and Set Design finals were scheduled back-to-back when I was an undergraduate in Ann Arbor.

*   *   *

At 5:45 p.m. I turn left off E. Palm Canyon and drive down the west side of Parker's landscaped grounds until I see the wardrobe trailers. Extras playing waiters and bartenders at the mythical country club had an earlier call. They hang out on the sidewalk wearing black trousers beneath long black aprons and goldenrod shirts with little logos that say "Dunes Club."

I park in a dusty dirt lot behind Parker's paved guest parking, where the white craft services tent has been moved from its previous downtown location. It is unseasonably cold and windy. Dust billows up from the dirt, mingling with the smoke surrounding the Mexican cooks who attend the barbecue grills containing tonight's dinner.

Parker began its life as a Holiday Inn in the 1960s and it retains a certain whiff of middle-brow mediocrity in spite of 500 thread count sheets and Jonathan Adler interior design. Adler took *Auntie Mame* as his inspiration for the hotel's makeover. The interiors of Parker's public spaces are supposed to recall the rooms Mame furnished with the treasures she collected on her worldwide travels. But the final result recalls something equally specific but geographically much closer. Parker's interiors look just like the collection of discards currently on display directly across the street from the resort at an estate sale company. In both venues, the eclectic mélange of styles creates an effect that might best be described as Salvation Army chic.

After my sport coat and trousers pass muster with my favorite costumer, an assistant director leads all the background players onto the set. We gather on the grounds of Parker immediately in front of the spa, where large letters over the entry read "P.S.Y.C." Parker intends the acronym as a geographic pun since a yacht club in the desert creates a presumably amusing oxymoron. But I see it in more psychiatric terms, envisioning famous and wealthy psychos, therapists, and patients all checking-in to reassure themselves about their own tenuous grasp on reality. This is, after all, the last place Robert Downey Jr. was arrested for possession of narcotics. It is also the place where Nicolas Cage (using the name Frankenstein Cadillac) checked in, and out of, the $5,000 per night

Gene Autry Suite after only a 20-minute stay. He was as impressed with the self-conscious and overpriced Parker as I am.

The manicured grounds in front of the P.S.Y.C. are set for an outdoor cocktail party. White floor-length tablecloths overlain with gold satin squares drape themselves around tall cocktail tables. Matching cloths decorate several low banquet tables that contain the buffet and serve as the bar for the party. Spotlights illuminate the area, masked by a variety of diffusers, but even with the heat from the lights, it is cold – very cold. Rain spits from darkening skies as we are led to the holding area for extras. Goosebumps and erect nipples abound.

Assembled in a banquet room, we receive instructions from the prop master, a bear-like man of indeterminate age.

"Tonight you'll be given drinks to hold, but they are props. Do not drink them. Repeat. Do not drink them. You may take a sip but no more. We won't be doing refills. The wine is grape juice. In a minute, we'll be setting up a table for you to put your drinks on when you return to this room between takes. The table is divided into squares and each square is numbered. Make sure you put your drink on the same square each time. Remember the number of your square and that way we won't have any trouble with people picking up the wrong drink. Okay?"

The prop master leaves and he is replaced by a dictatorial female assistant director, clearly inspired by the television commercial for Head On.

"We will be shooting all night tonight. Is there anyone who can't stay all night? We will be shooting all night tonight. Is there anyone who can't stay all night? We will be shooting all night tonight. Is there anyone who can't stay all night?"

Hearing no protest, the agent provocateur moves on.

"Okay. Now remember, it's a hot summer evening in Palm Springs and you've been spending the day around the pool. Now you're attending a cocktail party. It's warm and you're having a wonderful time."

That, under the circumstances, will require acting.

"No talking out loud on the set," she continues. "You will be pretending to talk to each other, but do it in pantomime. Stay on the paths and do not cut through the bushes. There are cables everywhere so be careful not to trip. Now let's go out to the set."

Once on the set, I notice that Handley and Heard are back for a second night, as are Gayle O'Grady, Sharon Lawrence from *N.Y.P.D. Blue*, and adorable gay munchkin, Leslie Jordan. Jordan is in his fifties, 4'11" tall, and his mischievous grin and endearing demeanor make people laugh even when he isn't speaking. Playing a waiter at the country club, Jordan is the only star on the set who chats with the extras.

After a few takes the rain starts to come down in earnest and we're quickly led off the set and back to the staging area. As soon as we're seated, a production assistant enters the room.

"You all have to move," she explains. "We need to move the equipment into this room because it's closest to the set. Bring your things and follow me."

None of us takes this personally. We understand the value of the lights and cameras on the set probably exceeds the net worth of most individuals in background. Yet I'm aware the 35 millimeter Panavision cameras, elaborate lights and sound equipment, and assistants who still use tape measures to accurately assess the distance between the star and the camera for purposes of a close-up are all no longer necessary. This pilot could be shot digitally with less than half of the equipment and crew for a quarter of the cost. But the motion picture business is slow to change, despite available technology. Every employee group is represented by a union quick to raise hell when a job is threatened. So the bloated, labor-intensive method of capturing dramas on film remains essentially as it was 75 years ago. The old adage, "the more things change, the more the stay the same" has special meaning in Hollywood. No one wants to buck the system because there is a paycheck or a percentage attached to every function on set or behind the scenes.

About 50 extras all pick up their coats and bags for the move to Parker's employee break room which features candy and soda machines and a locked wine storage cabinet. Two matching signs on the wall reflect the division of Parker employees into the "orange team" and the "yellow team." According a big zero written in magic marker, neither team has had an on-the-job injury this month.

Because of the rain director Scott Winant calls an early dinner break and we head for the craft services tent and the extra's food line. As with the night before, the extras get heavy pastas, potatoes, beef, and fried chicken staples. The cast and crew are already inside the tent partaking of a more refined selection of prime rib, salads, and pastries. Once the principal actors and crew are seated and fed extras are allowed to take plates and pick up servings of whatever remains at the cast and crew's banquet tables.

The stars travel in a little bubble of their own, separated by physical beauty, wardrobe, hair and make-up. Each and every one is, if not exceptionally handsome, extremely well groomed. And the twentysomething stars - black or white, male or female - are adorable. The contrast between the principal actors and the crew is even more startling because the crew of the "Untitled Kevin Williamson Project" is rather blue collar, to put it politely. They have bad teeth and hair, lousy clothes, and lumpen bodies. They are also really nice and they acquit themselves admirably while on the set. The only half-way attractive man on the crew is the tall, Clark Kent-like grip who carries the boom microphone. Between takes he spends most of his time hitting on the prettiest female extras.

When I sit down to eat, two guys from the crew are finishing their meals directly across from me at the long family-style table. I catch only the final fragment of their conversation, as one man turns to the other and volunteers, "Yeah, but now I find out I'm going to jail. It would be a lot easier to take if I didn't know I was going to have to go to jail."

After the 30-minute dinner break we return to the staging area and are quickly called to the set for the next scene. The rain stops, but in an uncharacteristic desert phenomenon, the air remains thick with the smell of it. A rare and seductive aroma floats on cold breezes, mixing with the fragrance of the orange blossoms on the trees scattered throughout the grounds. This heady perfume causes the set to take on the unmistakable feel of a tropical island suffering from a cold snap; the evening now seems fecund and full of promise.

Before the cameras roll, Winant reminds the extras, "Don't forget, it's a balmy summer evening and we're soon going to head off to the pool."

One of the extras turns to me, "You should have been there two nights ago, when Handley and Heard had to run around the golf course in the middle of the night while they turned the sprinklers on. We all deserve hazard pay for this."

It is 3 a.m. and we've been working since 6 p.m. We're freezing. The women have it worse than the men, because they complied with the request to wear high-heeled sandals and skimpy dresses. The rain returns, spritzing the cocktail tables with tiny ice pellets as mold grows along the surface of the liquid inside the extra's wine glasses. Everyone dons heavy coats during set-ups. The stars have attendants who hold umbrellas over their heads between takes. Their overcoats are whisked away by crew members when the assistant director announces, "camera is rolling." For the next three hours, we repeatedly hear the chant, "Background reset to one...... Camera is rolling..... Action!"

Our hot summer pool party finally breaks up at 6:20 a.m. when sunrise makes it no longer possible to get an evening shot. By this time all of us in background could walk straight onto the set of *Night of the Living Dead* and be perfectly in character. On this final day of shooting for the pilot we have worked over 12 hours. It will be months before I see the edited episode on YouTube, briefly recognizing my plaid shorts in one scene and finding my face, in profile, at the cocktail party.

The desert proves to be amazingly photogenic when the debut episode finally airs on May 30, 2007 on the CW Network. Now called *Hidden Palms*, the show is essentially *The O.C.* meets *Desperate Housewives* in Palm Springs. But there is one significant difference between the episode posted on YouTube and the one that finally airs. The original edit contained an interracial married couple waking up in bed one morning, stretching and moaning in contentment as the camera pulls back to reveal a handsome male companion simultaneously waking up beside them in the same bed. This one moment gave the debut episode an edginess conspicuously absent in the cut that finally aired. I would be willing to bet CW network executives considered this sort of bisexual ménage a bit too much for a prime time premiere.

As far as the Palm Springs Chamber of Commerce is concerned there is another fly in this ointment: for economic reasons, *Hidden Palms* will be shot using Phoenix as a substitute for Palm Springs.

POSTCARD

(1930-1955)

In the 1930s my parents migrate north from Tennessee to Detroit during the Depression to find work in factories. Carthage, Tennessee, their hometown and the home of my distant cousin, Al Gore, is a small town with few opportunities. Lacking even a high school education my parents' options are limited. Despite my mother's desire for a large family, after four miscarriages she finally gives birth to me, her only child, at the age of 41.

Once my mother achieves the goal of motherhood she stops working to focus all her energies on parenting. My continued existence in a healthy state is her only requirement for happiness. My father comes to feel differently.

In the 1950s, my mother looks like Doris Day in *The Man Who Knew Too Much*. Her natural black hair grays early and the label on the bottle of L'Oreal toner she carries to hairdressing appointments describes her preferred tint as "champagne beige." With green eyes and fair skin, she makes a stunning blonde in her fitted suits and t-strap heels. My mother's family is an old one; my grandfather was born during the Civil War. But after my mother is accepted as a member of the Daughters of the American Revolution she never attends a meeting. My overweight father is Archie Bunker with a southern accent. I will become the bane of his existence.

Skinny, effeminate, and contemplative by nature, I am none of the things my father's son was supposed to be. I am an alien creature to him, a boy who hates sports, enjoys reading, and plays with dolls. Adding insult to injury, I also steal the time and attention my mother once reserved for him. This is never a formula for familial success. Minor skirmishes on the battlefield of wills occur almost daily. Major battles are frequent. Given the imbalance of power and unequal allocation of resources, no child can prevail in such wars.

-2-

The Queer Museum

Little Bill, a city dog at heart, loves his twice daily walks from my house in Palm Springs. Although the back yard is large enough to accommodate his needs, it is used only for emergency deposits. Bill's walks lead us away from my house and into the gay twilight zone of the Warm Sands hotel district.

One of Palm Springs' older neighborhoods, Warm Sands is a mixture of single-family dwellings, apartment buildings, and commercial strips. It contains the first residential land tracts established in the 1920s for the construction of homes. It is also queer central for gay travelers and residents alike. My house is only one block from eleven resorts that cater to gay men. All the resorts are "clothing optional" and a few of them allow men to pay a day fee and hang out around the pool with other naked guys. There is also a fairly regular flow of cars that pass slowly through the neighborhood in repetitive circles, all driven by single male drivers who make frequent stops to meet new friends.

The neighborhood does not exist in a vacuum but it has adopted a distinctly Las Vegas attitude along the lines of "what happens in Warm Sands stays in Warm Sands." Just north of the Warm Sands hotel zone on Ramon Road, there is an architectural monstrosity that serves as a Catholic Church. Its corner marquee displays rotating aphorisms like "I'm a really good listener. – God"; "I exist. Therefore you are. – God"; and my personal favorite: "A dusty Bible means a dirty life." Just east of the Warm Sands border on Sunrise, there is a conservative Christian church which also operates its own private high school on an adjacent parcel of land.

I am accustomed to taking Little Bill on his evening walk right after his dinner of kibble mixed with half a baked potato. Bill loves his dinners, but not as much as he loves his walks. It is late afternoon and the weather is cool but brilliantly sunny and clear. The sun has set behind the San Jacinto Mountains and they sky is illuminated by a soft ambient light that seems to come from nowhere in particular. It is peaceful and quiet in Warm Sands.

Looking north toward the San Gorgonio pass, you can still see sunshine falling on the purple mountain peaks that now cast shadows across the valley. This is the desert's answer to the famous "magic hour" cherished by filmmakers. Here in the valley it is the time after the sun drops below the mountain peaks and before it sets in the west. The timing varies depending on the season and how far away you are from the San Jacinto Mountains. The further east you go, the more sunshine you get. The closer you are to the base of the San Jacinto Mountains, the earlier you are in shade.

Wearing threadbare jeans, a white sleeveless t-shirt, and a pair of clunky brown Skechers slip-ons that look positively orthopedic, I put Bill on his leash and walk out my front door. Bill leads me east toward the hotel zone. This evening there are more cars on patrol than usual, and after starting and stopping for Bill to retrieve messages at every mailbox and telephone poll, I notice one of the circling cars keeps coming back in my direction. It's a small Thunderbird nouveau, the kind Adrianna owned in *The Sopranos* until they drove her out into the woods and riddled her body with bullets as she screamed for mercy.

The car slows and the driver's heavily lidded eyes peer out beneath the protection of his black canvas roofline. He rolls down the passenger side window and, as Bill drags me forward, he silently pulls the car up until the driver's side door is beside me. The car, now at my side, proceeds at the same pace as my stroll. Glancing down into the passenger seat I see the driver behind the wheel is

completely naked and sporting a roaring hard-on. With the
assistance of a black leather cock ring, his dick springs
stiffly upward from a groin completely devoid of pubic
hair. At the base of his penis the scrotum drapes like a
puddle of skin around the family jewels. The driver's
engorged cock is larger than average and dusty rose in
color – the nice sort of pink one commonly encounters in
rubber products. The entire genital ensemble is perfectly
color coordinated, like the carefully painted face of a
dowager who slapped on a leather choker and stopped by
the Charles of the Ritz counter at Macy's for a
complementary makeover before heading out for
cocktails. It's also clear from what I can see of the driver's
face, he – like I - will not see 55 again.

I stand in the middle of the street, sporting a two-
day growth of beard, wearing a wife beater and jeans and
looking as unattractive as possible. In one hand I hold a
16-pound Lhasa Apso at the end of a leash and in the
other I carry a plastic bag full of dog poop. Where, I muse,
is the erotic potential in this picture? In my mind the
Thunderbird becomes the gay equivalent of Stephen
King's Christine…with a penis. My head floods with
questions as the car continues to parallel our trajectory.

Just what does this silent apparition expect me to
do? Could he possibly find me attractive? And if he's so

ready for action, why doesn't he stop skulking beneath the shadows of his canvas roof and just put the top down? I consider making some sort of joke but decide gentlemen who present themselves in such a fashion are not out for laughs. Then it hits me: this has nothing to do with me. What we have here is an exhibitionist.

Once that light bulb goes on I'm both pissed and insulted. And truth be told, I'm more than a little embarrassed to find myself engaged in some self-congratulatory preening as a result of his attention. I give Bill's leash a jerk and do a fast 180 toward home. The Thunderbird parks at the corner and I can feel the occupant's eyes boring a hole in my back as Bill and I retreat into the Wild West sunset. A few hours later, while unloading the dishwasher, I mentally review my late afternoon encounter and burst out laughing.

*   *   *

As a new member of Palm Springs' World Gym, I continue working out four or five days a week as I have for years. World is located in a shopping center off Sunrise. The gym opened a few years ago in a space formerly occupied by an Albertson's supermarket. It is a big windowless cavern and a welcome haven from the relentless sunshine of the summer months. Surrounding the workout floor with its central running track and adjacent group exercise room, the owners have hung wonderful enlargements of old fitness magazine covers from the 1950s. There is something comforting about lying on the floor and doing stomach crunches while looking up at Mickey Hargitay's basket, circa 1955, prominently displayed in a pair of tight white swimming trunks.

The gym features an excellent sound system and a deejay booth occasionally staffed with live deejays during peak, after-work operating hours. Music videos from the World Gym Entertainment Network are the alternate music source for the gym but most members opt for their own iPods to avoid overdosing on Britney Spears, Janet Jackson, Jennifer Lopez, and more obscure pop icons like Kylie and Danni Minogue. Kylie and Danni are an older Australian version of Jessica and Ashley Simpson and I'm actually surprised anyone at the World Gym Entertainment Network has even heard of Danni Minogue. At this point down-under Danni is so last century.

World has typical ceiling-mounted television screens above the treadmills and a juice and espresso bar offering smoothies and energy drinks. It is the premier gay gym of Palm Springs with a membership profile that is probably 95% men and 95% gay. The Palm Springs gay crowd moved over to World from the existing Gold's Gym as soon as World opened.

Gold's is located by the airport and housed in a beautiful two-story facility obviously created by an architect. The treadmills and exercise room are on the second floor. While working on stationary bikes, elliptical trainers, or Stairmasters at Gold's, you can either watch the overhead television screens or look outside through ceiling-to-floor windows. The panoramic view from the second floor includes the mountains in the distance and, in the foreground, the runways of Palm Springs International Airport. Airplanes take off and land just a few feet away from the gym all day and night, providing members with a spectacular show at no extra charge.

Gold's does not have a juice bar, but the migration of the gay crowd to World can probably be explained by a business decision Gold's made in the late 1990s. Once upon a time, Gold's had a small sauna in the center of the men's locker room, opposite the showers. It was very popular with the gay clientele, so popular, so busy, and so active that management decided to remove it and fill the space with extra lockers. World Gym, with both a dry sauna and a wet steam room, started drawing the gay crowd away from Gold's as soon as it opened.

I have worked out in gay gyms for 27 years, even when out of town on vacation or business trips. At World, armed with my leather Harbinger lifting gloves, a towel and a t-shirt, I feel like Miss Indiana Jones, heading off on a gay anthropological mission. I learned long ago that if you want to take the measure of a new city you don't start with its museums and monuments but with its supermarkets and shopping centers. They will tell you much more about who lives there, and what they value, than anything you will find in Frommer's or a Michelin guide. If you want to find out about the gay male community, head straight to the nearest gay gym. World Gym is certainly a queer museum, although not all the exhibits on display are of museum quality.

The staff includes two men who advertise their services for rent via nude photos and profiles posted on the Internet. A third man is a budding deejay and porn star, as thick in body as he seems to be in the head. A variety of personal trainers, both male and female, ply their trade as independent contractors, advertising themselves with glossy 8 x 10's and curriculum vitae that line the wall beside the men's locker room. And then there is the membership.

Young, hot guys are the exception at World. More often than not, guys who fall into this category are weekend revelers who descend upon Palm Springs for quick getaways and go to the gym to get their pump on before heading out for the bars or the darker corners of clothing-optional resorts. The regular membership skews toward the post-fifty crowd with some guys well into their seventies. Some are retired, others still work. Most of the older members are coupled, frequently in gay twin sets.

The phenomenon of the gay twin set intrigues me. It is something I have experienced from the inside looking out as well as the outside looking in. Once you understand its essential nature reentering the zone is difficult. Some gay couples are not only similar in age, but they look, dress, and talk alike. The thinking behind this sort of coupling, conscious or unconscious, goes something like this. He looks like me, he talks like me, and he acts like me – ipso facto – he validates all my choices and I find that so attractive. Since this person has made the same choices I have made, these choices must be wise and smart and I'm going to love him for making them. Doing so lets me love myself, both literally and by reflection.

It is difficult for these unions to survive the test of time. Based on a precise duplication of form, values, and tastes they usually fall victim to the unavoidable spoiler of all things temporal: change. Sooner or later one partner's needs, desires, or looks will change. This is when the other partner's once perfect self-reflection starts to resemble a fun house mirror. The equilibrium is thrown off and things go south. A change of venue is hard on these relationships and, at World, it is not uncommon to hear locker room banter about long-term relationships dissolving after relocating to the desert.

World Gym is certainly a hair-raising experience. I have never seen so many wigs, toupees, dye jobs, plugs, hair weaves, and comb-overs in one place. The gay senior crowd reflects the style sensibilities of the two Tony's, Bennett and Curtis, whose wigs always make me laugh out loud. But the younger members of World Gym are not exempt from the cringe-inducing fashion faux pas.

I always enjoy the guys I call the triplets of Belleville, a gay couple in lycra spandex who sport the same short platinum hair color and work out with a less attractive third guy with the same dye job. Then there are the two Realtors, a fiftyish couple with fairly nice bodies and average looks, who both have hair weaves executed in an identical shade of chestnut brown that reminds me of Susan Hayward in *Back Street*. One of them wears his weave in a standard short cut, with a fringe of bangs. The other has a modified pompadour, a big-haired weave that calls way too much attention to itself. Then there is the gay bumble bee, a man who is pushing sixty with a vengeance. His lean, beautifully muscled body is topped by a head that sports hair plugs in front. Unfortunately, he must have run out of money because beyond the kinky brown frontal fringe there lays a vast expanse of bald scalp. His gym outfit: black tank top and black and yellow striped spandex hot pants held up by wide black suspenders.

Nothing, however, quite compares to the guy I call pump daddy. One bald gentleman, well over the age of sixty, works regularly with a personal trainer. He begins his workout by walking around the World Gym track many times in his black spandex hot pants. Spandex for men over sixty is always a dicey proposition, but in the case of pump daddy, it is clearly a matter of pride. Obviously he uses a dick pump regularly and injects saline solution into his scrotal sac. The result of his practice, a fetish among a small number of both gay and straight men, is visually startling. Pump daddy proudly struts around the World Gym track like a gay Edy Williams, looking as if he's stuffed a cantaloupe down the front of his hot pants.

These exhibits in Palm Springs' queer museum are my gym entertainment, which comes without a cover charge. I have no problem with most of the men at the gym; some have become friends. Most are guys like me who have worked out for years and are trying to stay fit or at least keep their sagging butts from hitting the pavement. There is, however, one final group that pushes my buttons big time.

Sex in gym saunas and steam rooms has been going on as long as I've been working out. Nothing short of replacing all gay men with pod people, like the ones from *Invasion of the Body Snatchers*, will ever stop it. But World Gym has its own special group of guys who put the sex in sexagenarian. There is a group of older, morbidly obese men who rarely work out, but hang out in the steam or sauna and play with themselves, trying to scare up a little action. As if by some miracle of digital manipulation, they can take something that resembles a shitake mushroom and turn it into a Chinese cucumber - or that a casual observer might find these efforts sexually stimulating. This pushes my "ee-uuw" factor off the charts.

Yet I must confess if hunky, muscular young studs were engaged in the same behavior I would feel completely different. Do I have a double standard? Am I ageist? Am I repulsed by morbid obesity? We all have issues, and it's beginning to look like many of mine are featured entrees on the Palm Springs smorgasbord.

-3-

Night in the City

The day after my encounter with "Christine" I'm browsing through one of the local gay weeklies, the *Desert Daily Guide*, when I see an ad for the Tool Shed, Palm Springs' one and only "Leather/Levi Cruise Bar." It is located in the Warm Sands strip mall next door to Builder's Supply which is now part of the Ace Hardware chain. Many of the employees at Builder's Supply are gay, as are most of the patrons.

In numerous drive-bys I've already completed my mental mapping of the territory that lies just down the road from my house. The Tool Shed is made up of two storefronts with an adjacent outdoor patio. The business just east of the bar is Q Trading, a gay bookstore, video, greeting card, clothing, and chotchke emporium that occupies three storefronts. It is owned by two guys who once owned one of the Warm Sands resorts. Next to Q Trading, there is an antique store and an "all natural" bakery that makes and sells dog treats. At the far end of this collection of storefronts, there is a Hispanic meat market. I should probably clarify that this market actually retails beef and pork products. But this strictly heterosexual venue's claim to mainstream legitimacy is thrown strangely off kilter by the store's unfortunate name: The Cocula Meat Market. Go figure.

Perusing the ad in the *Desert Daily Guide*, I discover that tonight the Tool Shed is sponsoring an "RHSD - Red Hankies Sand (sic) Diego - Beverage Benefit." Those unfamiliar with the gay tradition of colored hankies may not be aware that men who sport red hankies dangling from the rear pockets of their jeans are people who receive sexual gratification through a fist shoved up an anus. If the hanky is worn on the left side, the person identifies as the dominant partner; if the hankie is placed on the right side, the person is receptive. I do not gravitate toward this particular sexual practice, and having seen it performed I cannot explain its attraction to anyone. I do find it somewhat curious that a Palm Springs bar is sponsoring a "Beverage Benefit" for men from "Sand" Diego who want to place their fists up men's anuses. Do the proceeds go toward towels and latex gloves? Is there a reserve fund for emergency proctology? In any case, the benefit tonight is from 7 to 10 p.m. I will be elsewhere.

The same full-page ad contains the bar's weekly calendar and it includes a deejay who spins retro records and remixes Friday through Sunday evenings. Sunday mornings from 6 a.m. to 2 p.m. there is "Church with the Church Lady" – a hosted gathering for those who have partied all night on Saturday and haven't had enough. On Friday evenings, in addition to the deejay spinning the hits of yesteryear, the Tool Shed proudly announces there will be a "Boot Pig on Duty."

Thursday evenings there is a pool tournament; Saturday afternoons at the Tool Shed are reserved for guys who want to drink brewskies while wearing black engineer boots and black leather boxer shorts; and Wednesdays from 9 p.m. are known as "Wet Wednesdays." The advertisement below the Wednesday night headline suggests, "Wear your yellow hanky!" Hanky placement for dominant and submissive positions follows the methodology described above, but in this case the desired activity of the hanky-wearer involves urination. You can choose to piss or be pissed upon and devotees of this practice are known colloquially as "golden shower queens," hence the Tool Shed's sponsorship of "Wet Wednesdays." God I love a parade.

At the risk of turning into Andy Rooney on an episode of *60 Minutes*, I feel I must confess my own personal love affair with leather. I have always worn leather belts. They hold up my pants. In 1978 I bought the most fabulous leather jacket. It was navy blue lambskin and it fit, and felt, like a soft glove. I have never loved a jacket as much as I loved that one. I now own not one, but two suede jackets. The older one is dark green and matches my eyes perfectly. It is made by Golden Bear in San Francisco. I bought it almost ten years ago and although worn and stained, it has the familiar lived-in feel of an old shoe and I have no intention of parting with it. The other jacket is a newer, blue-gray Jhane Barnes that I bought at the Cabazon outlet mall two years ago. I also own several pairs of leather shoes, none of which compares to the spectacularly comfortable taupe suede Ferragamo driving shoes I reluctantly discarded last year after wearing a hole through the soles. That, in short, is my personal experience of leather. I do not believe it makes me part of a community. It certainly doesn't make my dick hard.

I simply do not understand cowhide as a sexual fetish. But these are my peeps and I fully support freedom of sexual expression between consenting adults. There is, however, one evening in the advertisement for the Tool Shed's weekly offerings that I do understand. Monday nights at 9 p.m. the bar hosts "O-69 Bingo – Always Fun, Always Free!" Bingo - now that's something I understand. But what to wear?

Preparing for my leather bar debut, I rummage through my closet and come up with Levi's and a V-neck, short-sleeved black cotton sweater from Banana Republic. It does not approximate Marlon Brando in *The Wild Bunch*, but no amount of wardrobe could produce that sort of transformation. I do not own boots and I rule out my dorky white tennis shoes just before I realize that I'm obsessing.

I throw on some black socks and the beat-up brown loafers which served me so well on my recent encounter with Christine. They are unquestionably the wrong choice for this venue, I mean....brown loafers in a leather bar? They are the weirdest pair of shoes I own but also the most comfortable. They have no laces, buckles, or stitching and they look like something Frodo would wear to tramp around the forest in *Lord of the Rings*. With their rounded toes and thick soles, I walk like I'm balanced precariously on top of a couple of cow pies. Good. Fine. Perfect.

It's cold when I grab my green suede jacket and head out the door. I could walk the four blocks to the Tool Shed, but as far as I can tell, no one walks four blocks at a stretch in Palm Springs except for Darlene Rocky, the town's 66-pound anorexic who walks 20 miles a day all over town when she isn't doing guest shots on Dr. Phil.

As I emerge from my car in front of the Tool Shed I notice the ceiling-to-floor glass walls that constitute the eastern façade of the bar are blacked out so no one can see in or out. A swinging glass entry door opens to a leather curtain that maintains the absolute privacy of the inner sanctum. The thumping strains of Dan Hartman's 1978 disco hit, "Instant Replay," waft out into the night as I part the black leather drape and step inside. As soon as I part the curtain the music immediately stops and the lights inside the bar go up.

All right motherfuckers. It's green suede, and yes, the shoes are brown. If you don't like it you can all suck my dick on the steps of City Hall. My self-conscious mental defense ends as soon as I realize no one has noticed me. All eyes are focused on paper Bingo cards each man has in front of him; the end of the Dan Hartman fanfare evidently indicates the games are about to begin. I take a seat at the bar while a morbidly obese guy with a microphone sits down at a card table and spins the wheel of a wire basket before pulling the first number.

In his black leather cap, white t-shirt, and Birkenstocks, he shouts, "N-24," in a gravelly voice that could make Harvey Fierstein seem like Brittany Spears.

The bald, shirtless bartender saunters over to me, nipples erect.

"Hey, sweetheart, what can I get you?"

"A Diet Coke," I reply, somewhat taken aback by his genuinely cordial greeting.

The bartender fills a plastic beer stein from the syrup and soda hose and sets the drink in front of me.

"That'll be one seventy-five."

I plop down two bucks and start checking out the room. The u-shaped bar straddles the dividing line between the two storefronts that constitute the Tool Shed. Walls and ceiling are black, and silver chains - seemingly arranged in haphazard fashion - dangle from hooks overhead. As I scan the room I discover a crowd of about 60 men and no women. Less than six guys appear under the age of 50. Most seem to hover somewhere between Medicare and death and their wardrobe falls into the generic Levi and boots category. Many men wear black engineer caps, no shirt, and a leather vest that does nothing to hide stomachs that hang over belts. There is a smattering of flannel, black t-shirts, and salt & pepper topiaries trimmed into moustaches or goatees. The artifice of monochromatic dyed hair is frequently betrayed by its contrast against wrinkled skin.

The bingo caller shouts into the microphone, "B-10."

A spontaneous chorus of well-rehearsed players replies, "Put on your leather and pretend you're butch, Rocky."

I can hardly believe my ears. How long have these guys been rehearsing? When the next number is called the phenomenon repeats itself.

"I-18."

"You ate a teen?" queries the Greek or French, active or passive, chorus of players.

A few more numbers are called, some without rejoinder, as I glance about the room. Rainbow flags adorn one wall while other walls feature photos of guys in leather. Some photographs are of young professional models and others are group shots of members from the Palm Springs Leather Order of the Desert. Without their leather wardrobe the local members of the P.S.L.O.D. contingent could be contestants in a Fred Mertz look-alike contest.

"O-64," shouts the caller. "What do you call 64 in Palm Springs?"

"Chicken," replies the crowd without hesitation.

A framed poster from San Francisco's now defunct Bulldog Baths hangs nearby and a lighted case at the back of the bar contains cock rings, lube, black leather vests, and other accessories for sale.

"O-66," shouts the caller in an ahoy-matey, shiver-me-timbers baritone.

"Get your tricks on O-66," adds the chorus.

Patrons are scattered throughout the bar, perched on barstools, but the center of conviviality seems to be a gang of 13 men seated in white plastic garden chairs around a large table sheathed in black leatherette. Looking closely, I realize this is a pool table with a temporary cover. A large cardboard box in the middle of the table contains the blotters player use to color the numbers on their Bingo cards as they are called.

"B-11."

"And have lots of friends!"

"B-14."

"And hurt that asshole!"

"O-69!"

The bar erupts in cheers. This is not only a Bingo number but the name of the Tool Shed's Bingo evenings. The bartender scurries over to the waiters' station and starts lining up shot glasses. All Bingo action stops while he furiously fills orders for one dollar shots of the three featured libations: something labeled "Cactus Juice," a mango liquor, and Peppermint Schnapps. This fire sale begins only when the caller pulls "O-69" from the little metal hamper. A handful of guys lounging on the outdoor smoking patio but not playing Bingo, rush the bar when they hear the collective cheer. Once all orders are filled the bartender gives the caller a heads-up and Bingo resumes.

"B-9," he growls.

"The tests results came back and they were benign," the crowd replies.

"Bingo," shouts a guy from the gang of 13, as he moves toward the caller with his winning card.

The caller leans forward to scrutinize the card and announces, "We have a valid Bingo."

The winner chooses an envelope from a collection that is tacked to a pegboard and hands it to the caller. Like a movie star opening an Oscar ballot, the caller pulls out the card, reads it, then reaches into a bag to retrieve the prize specified: a large black dildo. Waiving his prize overhead, the winner returns to the table and a sexagenarian Bingo runner quickly sweeps the room picking up losing cards and passing out new ones.

He asks me, "Do you want to play?"

"Sure."

The runner hands me a card and blotter and I realize that although I understand Bingo in concept, I'm unclear on its execution. The guy sitting next to me cordially volunteers the answers to my questions.

"There are three boards on each sheet," he points out. "You play all three boards at once. These five vertical columns are labeled B, I, N, G, and O. You can't see that because the writing's too small, but that's what they are. But if you don't hear the letter, it doesn't matter 'cause the Bs are the small numbers and the numbers get larger as you go toward to the O column."

"So, do I have a Bingo when I get five numbers to line up vertically or horizontally?"

"Sometimes. Every game is different. If they call 'top and bottom,' you have to get the numbers in the top and the bottom row. If it's 'black out,' you need to fill one whole board. T and X are pretty obvious. Then there's 'double postage stamp' which means you have to get two blocks of four numbers on the same board. It's easy. You'll get the hang of it."

"Thanks," I reply, hoisting a blotter and preparing for battle.

My first game segues into a second, then a third — all without winning. Other players walk off with prizes like a haircut at the Palm Springs Barber Shop or a big black butt plug. The winner of the fourth game receives a green stuffed Easter Bunny which he takes back to the gang of

13. A fellow player places it face down and props the black dildo against the rabbit's ass. The game continues.

"B-8!"

"I looooove to be ate," shouts the crowd in perfect unison.

"B-4."

"Before you leave, don't forget to tip the bartender."

"Bingo!"

After validating the latest winner the caller decides it's time for a break. The music returns with Chaka Kahn's "I'm Every Woman." Guys head off for a bathroom break or outside for a cigarette and the bartender comes over to see if I need more liquid. I've polished off only one Diet Coke and one shot of Peppermint Schnapps all evening.

"Would you like a glass of water?" he offers sweetly.

"Thanks. That's a great idea. How about a club soda with lime?"

"You got it."

I look down at my newly delivered carbonated water and out of the darkness a man appears behind me and to my right.

"Is anyone sitting here?" he inquires, looking down at the adjacent empty bar stool.

"No."

But my visitor continues to stand, positioning himself well inside my comfort zone. One glance suggests the man is somewhere around sixty. He is clean shaven with a noticeably round face and a long pony tail. Strands of straight hair hang loose in front of his ears and his upper body careens from side to side as he reaches for the Budweiser the bartender sets on the bar. The patron appears to be at least part American Indian. My new friend does not sit down or pick up his beer. He sounds like Lauren Bacall and smells like a sodden Marlboro man.

"I just got out of Betty Ford," he informs me.

"Looks like it didn't take," I reply calmly, pointing to the beer sitting in front of him.

"No hard liquor," he volunteers by way of clarification.

It crosses my mind that neither the Betty Ford Clinic, which is located a few miles away in Rancho Mirage, nor Mrs. Ford herself – who can also be found in Rancho Mirage – would give a recovering alcoholic a get-out-of-rehab-free card if they promise to limit themselves to beer alone. It also occurs to me this line of reasoning will get me nowhere. I nod silently hoping my silence will be taken for consent, if not agreement.

"I live just a few blocks away in a million dollar house," he volunteers. "It's near the old Loretta Young estate. They all know me here. They won't serve me anything but beer."

Although drunken repartee is something I usually avoid, I find I just can't help myself.

I ask, "What were you in Betty Ford for?"

"Valium, vicodin, and vodka," he slurs. "The three V's."

As he begins to lose his balance, my uninvited companion grabs my bicep to steady himself.

"Oh, my God. You're huge," he remarks, continuing to squeeze my bicep. "What arms you have!"

This happens to me with disconcerting frequency. I never took steroids or hormones, but after 27 years of regular weight-lifting, I have good muscle tone. Yet no one seems to notice. I must be giving off some sort of "oh, Mary" vibe because no one comments on my body until they happen to inadvertently grab my bicep. One friend I've known for years actually recoiled in astonishment when he put his hand on my upper arm at a party and jumped back as if he had just grabbed a hot poker. I guess it never occurred to him I might have a muscular body under my loose fitting shirts.

At the Tool Shed my new friend continues to manhandle my bicep. I move my arm away and pick up my club soda, hoping to deflect his attention.

"My arms only seem big after you've had a few beers," I suggest.

Planting his hand firmly behind my neck, he pulls my head toward his with surprising force. Hot beer breath dusts my cheek as he speaks.

"Oh, no," he insists. "I know these things. Where is your husband tonight?"

That one is a no-brainer.

"He's back at the house, keeping the home fires burning."

I wrestle my head from the grasp of his hand and my friend picks up his Budweiser. With a toss of his ponytail, he has one more thing he feels he must share before walking away.

"I met Mae West in 1972."

With this proclamation he follows a jagged path into the recesses of the Tool Shed.

Bingo resumes and after a few more rounds the last game is played. At precisely eleven o'clock the caller announces the end of the evening's entertainment. Most of the men in the bar get up from their chairs and move toward the exit with their prizes.

Even before the patrons depart, the bar back and the Bingo runner collect and remove all the white plastic chairs and Bingo paraphernalia. They peel the leatherette cover off the pool table, the lights go down, and the music comes up. Within five minutes, two guys are shooting pool and the ambiance of the leather bar returns to more predictable territory. Only the clicking collision of pool balls atop green felt punctuates the disco beat. Leaning against black walls in the half-light of low-voltage pin spots, aging homosexuals in leather offer their version of *Boys Gone Wild*, Palm Springs style.

The next morning I sip coffee and read the newspaper with Little Bill seated in my lap. A small item announces that Google has mapped the surface of Mars. The work of the cartographer is never done.

POSTCARD
(1959)

I am nine years-old. My father and his hunting buddy Ken return late from a weekend hunting expedition. They pull our family's green Oldsmobile 98 sedan into the driveway and park by the side door to the house. It is early evening and my mother and I, having already finished dinner, hear the sound of conversation and slamming car doors in the driveway. We walk outside to greet the hunters, fresh from their kill.

The fall air is brisk when my father opens the trunk of the car and proudly displays his trophies. With equal doses of horror and morbid fascination I scan the neat rows of dead animals, organized and sorted by size and type. There are pheasants, rabbits, squirrels, and Mallard ducks whose colorful plumage seems to deserve a more dignified bier than the floor of a trunk. My father and Ken are dividing up the kill when I notice a cardboard shoe box in the corner nestled between the spare tire and boxes of shotgun shells. It seems to be moving.

"What's that?" I ask, looking up at my father.

"Open it and find out," he suggests.

I gingerly pick up the box and lift the lid to find a frightened wild rabbit cowering inside, ears flattened against brown fur. I lift it out of the box and cradle the rabbit to my chest, holding it tight and stroking its back.

"The bird dog caught it," my father explains.

"Oh dad, can I keep it? Can I keep it?"

My father looks at my mother, who remains silent.

"What would you do with a rabbit like that? It's wild."

"We could get a cage for it. I'll feed it and take care of it, I promise. Oh, please, please."

"You can't keep a wild rabbit in a cage. Come on, now. Give it back to me," he insists.

My father takes the rabbit from my arms and puts it back in the shoe box.

"Come here," he orders. "I want to show you something."

Reaching his arm around the doorjamb and into our house, my father flips a switch, turning on the floodlight that illuminates our back yard. He walks from the driveway into the center of the yard carrying the boxed rabbit and I follow. My continuing pleas for permanent custody fall on deaf ears.

"Sit down," he insists.

I sit on the damp grass and my father reaches into the box and pulls out the rabbit. He wordlessly begins to strangle it as I watch horrified.

"Stop! Stop! You're killing it. Stop, dad. Please stop!"

I reach for my father's arms but they elude my grasp. As the rabbit's eyes bulge and his hind legs paw frantically against my father's forearms I scream and cry for mercy. By the time the rabbit no longer shows signs of life I am sobbing uncontrollably. I run from where my father kneels in the yard, past the place where my mother and Ken stand in the driveway, and upstairs to my room. I throw myself on my bed and cry into my pillow until I have no more tears left.

Between sobs I hear my mother screaming at my father using words like "cruel" and "hateful" and asking for some sort of explanation as to why he would do such a thing. I can still hear my father's succinct answer.

"It'll make a man out of him."

The next night I am called to dinner, still sullen and heartbroken. In the middle of the kitchen table, per my father's request, a large serving platter contains the evening's entrée: rabbit. I can feel the anger and resentment inside my mother but she says nothing. I sit for only a moment before the combination of nausea and tears forces me to retreat once again to the solitude of my room.

-4-

Hollywood in the Sand

World Gym is one of the few gathering places for gay men in Palm Springs that is neither a resort nor a bar. It is also the place you can find Earl Greenburg when he is in town, although you won't be able to talk to him. Greenburg arrives weekdays in the early morning to put in seven miles on the treadmill before heading off to Koffi for his 9:30 a.m. caffeine fix, frequently enjoyed while conducting business.

At the gym Greenburg does not mingle with other members or start conversations. I have never seen him in the locker room. He arrives swaddled in a sweatshirt with his Bose headphones beneath a baseball cap and a towel wrapped around his neck, finishing his workout looking like a sweatbox Daddy Warbucks. Pulling out of the parking lot, his new 7-series BMW infers the kind of money that gives resonance to the Daddy Warbucks comparison.

Greenburg is Palm Springs' most influential philanthropist and gay businessman. He and his partner of

10 years, David Peet, sponsor the Desert AIDS Project as well as helping fund low-cost housing for AIDS patients. He gives generously to many causes, sits on the boards of many companies, and appears with alarming regularity in the social pages.

For many years the multi-millionaire Greenburg was a Hollywood "suit" as director of daytime programming for NBC. Trained as an attorney, Greenburg, now 60, broke out of the network box first with infomercials, then as president of the Home Shopping Network, and finally with a phenomenally lucrative little syndicated show known as *World's Wildest Police Chases*. He came up with that simple, and simply brilliant idea while watching the L.A.P.D. chase O.J. Simpson down the freeway in the notorious Ford Bronco. He is also the Chairman of the Board of the Palm Springs Film Festival.

I really want to like Earl Greenburg and I'm pleased when he agrees to meet me at Koffi, an extremely popular hangout for everyone gay and many who are not. In the shadow of the looming San Jacinto Mountains, the coffee shop opens onto a large, enclosed garden off North Palm Canyon. Greenburg insists on a table in the shade. A bout with malignant melanoma put the fear of God and sunshine into him a few years ago. But he loves Palm

Springs and lives and works here full time, except for the summer months when he and his partner retreat to their home in Connecticut.

"I like it here in the summer," he clarifies, "but David doesn't so we live in Connecticut for those months. Otherwise we live here in Palm Springs in the same house I've lived in since 1988."

Greenburg has an adult son and daughter by his ex-wife; the daughter is a lesbian. And he and David Peet plan to have a child of their own this year, using a surrogate mother.

The timing of this choice is so exceptional, I have to ask.

"Earl, what are you thinking? A new baby at sixty? Why are you taking on that sort of responsibility at your age?"

"Well you know what they say; a new baby buys you another ten years."

His answer takes me off guard and I quickly connect the dots that join cancer with sixty and lead to a heightened sense of one's own mortality.

Greenburg still has his own marketing and development firm and is quite a character, one made more interesting by his average height and unprepossessing physical persona. Dressed casually in a yellow cotton shirt and chinos, he carries more weight around his middle than he should, and he knows it. We are not chums nor will our relationship ever evolve into one of casual camaraderie. For that to happen I would somehow need to bridge a gap of at least $50 million.

Getting right to the point I ask, "As Chairman of the Board of the Palm Springs Film Festival, what do you do?"

"I'm unpaid but I got involved in the festival four years ago when it was coming out of a period of tremendous conflict. One of my best friends here had put a lot of money into it to revive it. I agreed to participate only if I could replace the Board of Directors. It's now made up of a diverse cross section of the whole valley, a lot of people who have made major contributions to the festival to get it back on its feet."

"Financial?"

"Yes, financial. If you're going to be on a board you have to either give money yourself or go out and raise it. There's also a third category, which believe it or not is not as important because we have a great staff, but you can do stuff as well. There is a lot to do, but unless you want to give up your day job you can't do that much. We have a few board members who do this. But it's easier for people who just write the checks. We've made it a more successful festival because we have totally focused on media exposure."

No one can quite pull focus like Greenburg. Although he successfully circumnavigates my question about his role as Chairman of the Board, it is apparent that together with his financial support, Greenburg is the man who gets movie stars to show up for the black tie gala awards presentation held at the Palm Springs Convention Center. Ticket sales for this one evening bring in as much money as the box office generates during the entire two weeks of film screenings.

"We don't book anyone unless they agree to show up," he acknowledges without hesitation. "We do it though the studios. The stars have contracts where they are required to publicize their films."

It doesn't hurt that the festival happens just at the time the annual race for Oscar gold starts to heat up. But the clout Greenburg brings to his position as Chairman is built on many years of Hollywood contacts, most of them in television.

"Why don't you write a biography or a memoir?"

"Many people have suggested that. I have a million stories but I can't tell them. I'll share one with you, so you understand why."

With this, Greenburg describes the time he was collared by his boss and ordered to go down to the musical director of a popular late-night talk show and tell him he had to stop selling cocaine to the show's famous stars. Most of the people in this story are still living.

"How could I tell that story in print? There are so many stories. When I was at NBC, I started out as head of daytime and there were eight game shows on the air. Five weeks later, there were two game shows on the air. I cancelled six. I kept *Jeopardy* and *Wheel of Fortune*. I'd like to think it was because I was brilliant but it wasn't. Truthfully it had nothing to do with my knowing they were big hits because they weren't big hits on the network. They became big hits in syndication.

"We started developing reality based programs and the one show I wanted really badly was a morning show on the local ABC station in Los Angeles. I think it was called *Regis and Sara Purcell* or *Regis and Cindy Garvey*. I forget now. I started courting Regis Philbin quietly because the local ABC affiliate was run at the time by a powerful guy named John Severino – a really scary guy.

"We finally got Regis to come to NBC and I remember the first day of his show. I got to be the executive producer despite the fact that I working for the network at the same time. I got a dead fish wrapped in newspaper."

"Oh my God," I exclaim. "That's right out of *The Godfather*."

"The truth is the thing was sent to Regis. But I felt really bad about that, so I said it was sent to me because Regis is a very sensitive guy. We knew it came from Severino. In any event, that was an interesting experience. What made it even more interesting is that we had to find a female co-host for the network version of the show and I went on a search. We found this woman named Mary Hart who to this day remains a dear friend. She also hosts our film festival awards ceremony. That's not by accident. I guess the nicest thing I ever did for her was get rid of her on the Regis show. She was actually too smart for him. I sent her over to a new show that was starting up called *Entertainment Tonight*. Now 25 years later, at about $20 million a year, Mary Hart is probably a very happy woman because she met me and I got rid of her."

I wonder what I'd have to do to have Greenburg to get rid of me in the same fashion. It's easy to see why Greenburg is the go-to guy in Palm Springs. If he can't make it happen personally he'll know someone who can, and despite his relatively transparent false modesty he clearly loves being the local mover and shaker.

"I've done over 100 infomercials but I don't produce stuff anymore. Well, every now and then I do because it's always in your blood, but what I do produce comes out of our Santa Monica office where I have a business partner. Instead of me doing the hundreds of thousands of miles of travel each year to meet with our clients, he does."

In the middle of his sentence Greenburg's cell phone rings and he looks at the display.

"Excuse me, I need to take this."

After a brief conversation in which he does lots of listening and little talking, he explains. "That was someone calling me from Atlanta. He's one of my non-clients who wants me to get a prototype of his product made in China and he has no money. I'm sitting here thinking, 'Why am I doing this?' I've tried to stop but I can't seem to."

I've known many highly successful individuals and they all seem to suffer from a similar problem: a difficulty in separating human begin from human doing. I have a feeling Greenburg is no exception. But the star power and financial success he brought to the Palm Springs Film Festival is not without its down side.

In the eyes of serious cineastes the festival is a lightweight. It doesn't discover new talent nor is it on the cutting edge. With its population of 45,000 Palm Springs is a small town; but it isn't Park City or Telluride. Unlike the annual Sundance and Telluride events, the Palm Springs festival is known primarily for tinsel. In a quid pro quo arrangement, Hollywood actors, directors, and film studios in pursuit of golden statues trade their participation for recognition. It is, in short, the star-fucker film fest, and the one I'm covering this year.

*   *   *

After many festival screenings I'm forced to accept that the "little pictures," made on a shoestring for the gay/lesbian audience, are a predictable lot. I dutifully sit through half a dozen offerings with the enthusiasm children reserve for taking vitamins. Between screenings, I meander over to Look, a gay restaurant downtown. My favorite waiter is a skinny black drag queen named Francois who can always be counted on for large doses of snap-queen attitude with every helping he delivers to the table.

"That Tommy Rose," he snorts. "She won't put me in her show."

"How come?"

"She says her Sunday night drag show at Toucan's has a fixed cast and it's already set. But every time that bitch puts together a benefit show, her regulars disappear, and who do you think she calls?"

"Let me guess."

"That's okay. I'll show her. I'm putting together my own show over at Streetbar."

Toucan's, a gay watering hole on the north end of town, is the drag venue de jour in Palm Springs. It draws a friendly gay crowd with entertainment that not only includes drag queens, but go-go boys, as well. The zaftig Tommy Rose puts on a good show, with lip-synching performers who actually seem to have heard the songs they're delivering. The continuing allure of this sort of spectacle eludes me.

"How come old school drag is so popular here in Palm Springs?"

"Oh, honey," Francois sighs, with eyes cast heavenward, "this town is starved for entertainment. So girlfriend, what'd you see at the film festival? Anything good?"

"Not much. But I had a priceless moment at a screening of *Sophie Scholl – The Final Days*."

"Sounds like a downer."

"Yeah, pretty much. It's a talky World War II courtroom drama, a true story about a girl and her brother who both get beheaded for being part of a German resistance movement called 'The White Rose.'"

"I hear that. I been resisting a white Rose myself, and it's about to kill me, too."

"But here's the funny thing. In the middle of the film Sophie's all upset 'cause she's afraid her arrest will freak out her poor old mom. She's an emotional wreck and practically bursting into tears when she explains the reason she's concerned about her mom: 'She's over 60!' That's when the audience burst out laughing?"

"How come?"

"At least half that crowd was packing a Medicare card. I don't think they felt 'over 60' should be a special cause for concern."

"Hmmm. Guess you had to be there."

"Yeah, well, never mind. But if you haven't seen *Brokeback Mountain*, you definitely should. It's playing at the festival but it's in general release, too."

*   *   *

The great gay hope from last year is *Brokeback Mountain*, an extraordinary and eloquent film that somehow managed to get studio backing and a major marketing campaign. Its star, Jake Gyllenhaal is being honored at the awards gala. Shirley MacLaine will also receive the festival's Lifetime Achievement Award and she's getting lots of bad press locally for being cantankerous and difficult. I meet one of the festival publicists responsible for keeping her happy at the festival's press room in the Wyndham Hotel. A young gay man, he just rolls his eyes when I ask if the stories are true.

"You should see the list of demands she submitted for what she wanted waiting in her suite," he adds sotto voce. With a little pleading I manage to wrangle a place on the red carpet for the festival's gala awards ceremony to be held at the newly expanded Palm Springs Convention Center and, at 4:30 in the afternoon, I stroll over to register at the press desk and stand in line with the rest of the press corps.

The paint is barely dry on the new addition to the convention center, but it makes quite an impression. A large swooping canopy, clad in copper, curves around the corner of the building and up over a formal entrance three-stories tall. The canopy is supported by columns clad in stone and the effect is sensational from both the street and the lobby, where a large glass wall faces the spectacular panorama of the San Jacinto Mountains. The building recalls the lodge in Hitchcock's *North by Northwest* where Cary Grant and Eva Marie Saint ran from Martin

Landau, scrambling down the mountain and onto the face of Mount Rushmore. But my good friend, The Architect, does not see the building in such a generous light. He thinks it is "decorative."

Those unfamiliar with the parlance of architects need to know that when an architect says a building is "decorative" what he really means is this: "That piece of crap is the equivalent of a chintz curtain draped over a vinyl window. It is so far below the standard of real architecture, it is simply beneath contempt." File that away.

I arrive at the a.) *beautiful* or b.) *decorative* façade of the convention center and check-in with the volunteers who maintain the press list. I'm given access to the red carpet only, and placed at the very end of the press line next to Croatian Television and two contest winners who wrote essays for KMIR-TV on why they wanted to be on the red carpet. I am not granted access to the award ceremony. It never ceases to amaze me when the alternative press is treated as a poor step-child by publicists. I am covering this event for the largest and oldest gay weekly newspaper in America, yet I find myself once again in the back of the bus.

This is happening in a year in which *Brokeback Mountain* is the top contender for the Oscar; Jake

Gyllenhaal (Brokeback) and Felicity Huffman (*Transamerica*) are being honored at the Palm Springs festival for playing a gay man and a transgendered woman respectively; Heath Ledger and Phillip Seymour Hoffman are the front runners for the Best Actor Oscar for playing gay men; the head of the film festival, Earl Greenburg, is gay; the mayor of Palm Springs is gay; and gay members hold a majority of the seats on the Palm Springs City Council. And I'm supposed to smile and handle this treatment with precisely the same equanimity that Prissy handled that post I-don't-know-nothin'-bout-birthin'-babies slap Scarlett dished out in *Gone With the Wind*. Well, shut my mouth.

Attendance at this year's festival is up 22% and big stars have flocked to the desert to accept or present awards. The winners are sent home with a bronze trophy somewhat taller than an Emmy and twice as weird. It's hard to determine exactly what the designer was going for but the statuette looks like an anorexic court jester juggling a bunch of tennis balls.

For tonight's function the organizers have two parallel red carpets that lead into the lobby of the convention center, both cordoned off by velvet ropes. The press is lined up behind the ropes along the southern red carpet. The northern red carpet, a few feet away, is intended for non-celebrities. Publicists sort the wheat from the chaff before they enter the front door with subtle directions to the appropriate line. The non-famous are directed to the far carpet, the famous are sent down the other side for interviews and photos.

I stand for three hours behind the ropes at the end of the celebrity red carpet. It is the point in the line where late-arriving stars get whisked away by handlers into the convention center for the gala award ceremony and dinner - the one I won't be attending. The biggest stars always arrive late and only make themselves available to the media representatives who can give them the most coverage. *Entertainment Tonight, E! Television, CNN,* and national networks take up most of the stars' time.

Celebrities whose time in the sun has not yet arrived or whose stardom is long past, arrive earlier and chat longer. On the red carpet tonight Tippi Hedren and Sally Kellerman stand out because of their remarkable class and graciousness. Both women look sensational and stop to talk with every reporter who wants a quick interview and some photographs or video footage. Hedren sports an attention-getting jeweled evening bag in the shape of a lion. She explains, "It was a gift from my daughter, Melanie (Griffith), who knew I would love it because of my work with lions at my animal sanctuary."

No-shows on the red carpet include Kathy Bates and Shirley MacLaine; the latter reportedly too ill to walk and speak at the same time. But MacLaine is not too ill to enter the convention center by the back door and accept her lifetime achievement award on stage with the other celebrities. Keanu Reeves, who presents Charlize Theron's award, is also a no-show on the red carpet reportedly for "security reasons" according to the publicist. Say what?

The diminutive Gary Sinise is friendly and open and Felicity Huffman, as she rushes into the auditorium, at least has the sensitivity to shout-out an apology to the press at the end of the red carpet, explaining she is the first person on stage and she's running late.

Croatian television quickly gets the message they've been shafted by their placement on the red carpet and the two bleached-blond female reporters and their cameraman (who showed up with his own step ladder) push their way up to the front of the line, positioning themselves behind reporters with better placement, hoping to shove a microphone through their ranks and get some sort of useable footage courtesy of their step ladder.

The disappearance of the Croatian contingent leaves me standing next to Fabio, from RAI Italian Television and his crew of three gay men who drove over from West Hollywood. Fabio is a hoot – tall, thin, with an incredibly goofy and endearing face that somehow vaguely recalls Pee Wee Herman – before his arrest. Fabio decides he will ask the ladies about the contents of their evening bags as they pass.

"Just wait. It's the only thing they'll use when they cut this footage together. I promise you." Some women cooperate, others do not. He does frequent shout-outs to celebrities who continually elude his grasp as they head toward their seats.

He calls optimistically after them, "How about a 'bon giorno' for Italian television?"

In concept it's a simple interrogatory, but celebrities hearing the request look back at Fabio and respond with a quizzical expression and the occasional bewildered smile and waive of the hand.

I end up camping it up and dishing with Fabio and his crew as celebrities like William H. Macy, Terence Howard, Peter Sarsgaard, Viggo Mortensen, Virginia Madsen, Mary Hart, Fionnula Flanagan, Charlize Theron, and Jake Gyllenhaal flash by. Theron, who I interviewed over a cup of coffee at San Francisco's Stanford Court Hotel two years ago, remains perfectly beautiful and impeccably turned out. Gyllenhaal is not quite as attractive in person as on screen, but the small crowd outside the convention center erupts into screams and applause for only his arrival.

Gyllenhaal is about six-feet tall and he has the traditional hallmark of the movie star: a big head on a small body. But the distance from the bottom of Gyllenhaal's ear to the tip of his chin is as long as the Baja California peninsula. In profile his exaggerated jaw line creates something of a marionette effect, as if God made some sort of assembly error on His production line and placed a bobble-head on top of a body too small to support it. But full-face Jake's a knockout.

Before Gyllenhaal enters the convention center Palm Springs Mayor Ron Oden walks down the red carpet with his frequent date, a 44-year-old interior designer I knew in San Francisco when he was the lover of a Realtor who worked at my firm. As a couple they were known for their kinky sexual practices and fondness for group encounters. On Manhunt.com, the mayor's date has naked pictures of himself and uses the handle, "PSmuscleBtmHottie." He describes himself as "6' 200 lb. Hard Muscle Btm guy. Passionate kisser. Big wired NIPS. Bottom guy with an edge." One of the photos shows his penis in a black leather cock ring and his balls extended by a matching leather ball stretcher. Recalling these photos I can't help but wonder if the mayor sees him because of, in spite of, or in ignorance of his web persona.

In the midst of my musings I look up and see Palm Springs resident Suzanne Somers and her husband Alan Hamill as they stroll by. Somers wears a beige satin bias cut gown covered by a matching satin paratrooper's jacket with huge puffy sleeves.

I nudge the male contest winner standing to my left, "Would you get a load of that jacket. What was she thinking?"

"Dollars," he replies.

"What do you mean? It looks cheap. That's the kind of jacket gay men wore in pea green with an orange lining, in the late seventies. I haven't seen anything like it since."

"Yeah but that's the kind of thing she sells on the Home Shopping Network, and she has to be seen in the clothes she sells. I heard her tell someone that each time she goes on HSN, she walks away with at least $250,000."

"How do you know this?"

"I worked a few catering jobs at her house in the Cahuilla Hills. It's an incredibly beautiful home spread out over the hillside on several levels. She lives next door to Barry Manilow and his partner. Actually, if you saw her home you'd know she has exquisite taste. And in person, she couldn't be sweeter."

At the conclusion of the red carpet parade the Croatians finally return to the back of the line to pack up their gear. All did not go well. The two female reporters bicker, spouting a stream of vitriolic gibberish that sounds Russian but is probably Serbo-Croatian. The cameraman distances himself from their argument, wisely avoiding the projectiles that would come his way if he interrupted the cat fight.

After receiving her Lifetime Achievement Award from Kathy Bates at the ceremony, Shirley MacLaine not only demonstrates she is able to walk and talk at the same time but willing to engage in more strenuous activities. She casts a glance in the direction of Charlize Theron and calls out, "Charlize, Room 204 – the three of us. Everyone else in this town is doing it!" This brief aside may be the most honest remark of the night. Although MacLaine says this is her first visit to Palm Springs in twenty years, she has put her pulse directly on the lifeline of what draws many people to "relax" here in the desert. Her take is right on target.

The following morning Palm Springs' newspaper of record, *The Desert Sun*, runs several lengthy stories on the gala. The paper, owned by the Gannett chain that also owns *USA Today*, is always full of typos and consists primarily of stories cut and pasted onto its pages from wire services like The Associated Press. Today the newspaper quotes presenter Peter Sarsgaard at the awards ceremony, speaking about his friend Jake Gyllenhaal, "His dogs are named Boo and Atticus. If that doesn't tell you who Jake is, I don't know what will. Jake grew up in a family that loves stories."

The helpful editorial staff of *The Desert Sun* adds the following explanatory note beneath the Sarsgaard quote, "Boo and Atticus were the children in Harper Lee's *To Kill a Mockingbird*." Anyone who reads or who saw Gregory Peck in the movie, can tell you that Atticus is the name of the kids' attorney father, and Boo is the name of the mentally challenged adult who lives near them. Yet I, as a lowly member of the alternative press, am the one shown to the back of the press bus.

Waiter, bring me a cup of hemlock – neat, no chaser.

*   *   *

At Oscar time the Best Picture award goes to *Crash*, a miserable, cliché-ridden, fag-free film about racism in Los Angeles. I hated the film so much when I saw it at a press screening, I told my editor it wasn't worth the space in the paper for a review. *Crash* is mean-spirited, shallow, unbelievable, and overwritten. On a nationally compiled list of the top 100 releases of the year critics collectively placed *Crash* in 66th position.

In the *Los Angeles Times* the morning after the Oscars, film critic Kenneth Turan intelligently and eloquently rips the academy a new asshole for failing to name *Brokeback Mountain* Best Picture. And although he did not use the word, he cited homophobia as the sole reason for this oversight. *Brokeback* was named Best Picture by The New York Film Critics Circle, the British Academy of Film and Television Arts, the Independent Spirit Awards, the Golden Globes, the Critic's Choice Awards, and the Venice Film Festival, among others. It just isn't quite good enough for The Academy.

As far as art is concerned, the Academy gives it lip service but they traditionally stand up and salute the middle-brow and mainstream. The box office success of *Brokeback Mountain* was a fluke. It will not open the floodgates for a stream of new gay-themed motion pictures because, in Hollywood, that dam is empty. Homosexuals will always be a minority, a minority many Americans still mistrust or despise. But contrary to commonly held beliefs, the issue here is not a moral one.

The wonderful actress Ellen Burstyn once told me, "Hollywood has no morals. If they thought they could make money portraying gay and lesbian people in a positive light, they would do it." Instead of morals Hollywood has accountants; films about gay people cannot provide the studios and the major corporations that now own them a guaranteed profit. For the rest of my life - and probably yours - homosexuals will remain on film exactly as we are in our society: marginalized. That's the simple truth.

-5-

Walking the Walk

Palm Springs remains enthralled by its past connection to Hollywood which lies just 100 miles west of the San Jacinto Mountains. Depending on your point of view, it wallows in reflected glory – real or imagined - or it actively invites a serious case of guilt by association. Movies stars began hiding out in Palm Springs in the 1920s, establishing a trend that, although not yet dead, is certainly on the wane. One of the city's older neighborhoods is the "movie colony" where many stars bought homes and quickly surrounded them with high walls and metal gates. The quiet charm of desert winters in a small town made Palm Springs an ideal get-away for quick rests or illicit movie star affairs, especially when international air travel was time-consuming and relatively primitive.

On the north end of town the tennis courts and swimming pool of the Palm Springs Racquet Club were a favorite hangout of movie stars through the 1950s. It is said Marilyn Monroe meet her Svengali, agent Johnny

Hyde, around the Racquet Club's pool. Wine, women and song – the latter often provided by Frank Sinatra – were the order of the day and bad behavior was not only tolerated but expected. The main party venue at the Racquet Club was the Bamboo Room, a restaurant and nightclub located adjacent to the swimming pool. The club was owned and operated by Charlie Farrell, a film actor who later became known for his role as Gale Storm's father on the 1950s television series *My Little Margie*.

The Racquet Club ultimately closed its doors. The pool, the Bamboo Room, and the guest cottages have now been empty and abandoned for years. The movie star crowd moved east to the gated enclaves of Rancho Mirage or stopped coming altogether. A newer condominium complex was added to the Racquet Club site and it now boasts a large gay population. The historic original facilities recently sold to a consortium that plans to add new condos, refurbish the Bamboo Room, and reinvent the property for a contemporary crowd. It is an ambitious undertaking.

Palm Springs' efforts at maintaining its Hollywood connection include the downtown Walk of Stars on Palm Canyon Boulevard as well as on Museum Way in front of the Palm Springs Art Museum. This transparent theft of an idea pioneered by the Hollywood Chamber of

Commerce on Hollywood Boulevard began here in 1992. Granite stars are set in concrete squares with a brass plaque containing the name of the famous or not-so-famous honoree that once lived or partied in Palm Springs.

Honorees on the Palm Springs Walk of Stars must have contributed to the charm, worldwide prominence, and name recognition of Greater Palm Springs in categories like show business, literature, civic duties, humanitarian efforts, sports, or military service. And like the Hollywood Boulevard walk, once the minimum criteria is met a star comes with a price tag. Almost 300 names decorate the Palm Springs Walk but the honorees are often considerably less famous than those found in Hollywood. It's hard to get too excited about a sidewalk that attempts to extract glamour from names like Kem Dibbs, Pierce Lyden, Andrew Fenady, and Velma Dawson.

In fact it has been conclusively established that even a monkey can have a star on the Palm Springs Walk of Fame. The monkey in question is Cheeta, the chimpanzee co-star of Johnny Weissmuller and Maureen O'Sullivan in the Tarzan films. Cheeta, now 75, is a Palm Springs resident who currently boards with the nephew of his original trainer. Cheeta occasionally makes local public appearances, like the art show I attended last summer at Studio One Eleven on Palm Canyon Drive. Cheeta the chimp is now an abstract painter and his work can be purchased at the gallery, with proceeds going to a non-profit. When he makes personal appearances, Cheeta is always kept on a chain by his handler, in clear view of his fans but out of reach. Seventy-five years of domestication can't guarantee the wild animal will not re-emerge and Cheeta is not petite. He is, however, diabetic.

When Cheeta makes personal appearances he is kept occupied by generous servings of his favorite snacks like popcorn and an endless supply of diet sodas which he swigs directly from the can. This afternoon as I walk past Cheeta's star at 110 S. Palm Canyon I find myself unexpectedly encouraged by one thought: if, at 75, a monkey can have a second career in Palm Springs, I don't know what the hell I'm worrying about. But Cheeta is not the reason I'm walking down Palm Canyon; the reason is Julius Shulman.

In the early '90s I was collaborating as co-author and co-photographer of a book about Los Angeles landmarks. The work was grueling because we had to research and photograph 575 different landmarks all over Los Angeles. The effort proved to be a revelation because it introduced me to many extraordinary buildings scattered around the city of angels and the great tradition of progressive architecture Los Angeles can rightly claim. By that time most of L.A.'s famous buildings were already documented in different books or periodicals, and the best images of these buildings were invariably captured by one photographer: Julius Shulman.

As a point of pride, or at least to justify our advance from the publisher, we felt we had an obligation to capture images not seen before. We wanted to come up with an original photographic point of view. Often the passage of time altered the buildings or their setting in ways that made this task easier. But with buildings that remained untouched or those that had been lovingly restored to their original condition, the definitive image was always one Julius Shulman already captured on film. He always showed the best angle in his perfectly composed images. Shulman's incredibly sophisticated eye consistently captured the spirit of the architecture in a way we could not improve upon.

Stepping lightly over Cheeta's star I head toward the corner of Palm Canyon Drive and Baristo. The day is a snowbird's delight with temperatures in the mid '60s and scattered high clouds floating above the mountains like cotton candy. The sky is turquoise and a light breeze blows from the west. It is shirt-sleeve weather.

Tourists in Bermuda shorts stroll slowly past shops and linger over late lunches at sidewalk cafes. The traffic on Palm Canyon reluctantly obeys the slow pace set by pedestrian-friendly stoplights. As I approach the corner building at 300 S. Palm Canyon, I see yellow police tape flickering in the distance. It curves out into the street, defining the area where white folding chairs cluster around a podium and spectators sit or stand, awaiting the formal presentation of the newest star on Palm Springs' Walk of Stars.

The handsome modernist building on the corner was designed by local architect E. Stewart Williams and built in 1960 as the Santa Fe Federal Savings Building. It currently serves as the offices of the Wessman Development Corporation and is owned by local developer John Wessman who hopes to transform the now tired façade of downtown Palm Springs with new retail and residential construction. I approach the gathering just as the first speaker takes the microphone and begins the dedication of the 256th star. A volunteer hands me a souvenir program for today's dedication and I notice the honoree, Julius Shulman, sitting in the front row. He is nattily turned out in a bottle green sweater vest and striped shirt, with salt-and-pepper hair pushed back from his high forehead. He still sports a small gray moustache

The 95-year-old architectural photographer patiently listens to a succession of local politicos, architects, and architectural historians as they extol his virtues. Mayor Ron Oden ends the series of speeches by presenting the honoree with a plaque proclaiming this as Julius Shulman Day in Palm Springs.

Assisted by his walking cane the honoree rises and stands behind the podium. Speaking in a clear voice with no hesitation, Shulman immediately proposes that all who have gathered to honor him should help him move his star just five miles south.

"It's only about a five-mile walk," Shulman optimistically suggests, "down to the Indian Canyons. And we can put this star in the pool of water I discovered when I first came to Palm Springs on a camping trip in August, 1926. I was 15-years-old and traveling with five members of my high school gymnastics team. At that time Palm Springs had a population of about 1,200 and most of them were Indians. They were friendly and I got to know them. They took me around and showed me places."

Shulman no longer moves well but his mind is as alert as ever. He goes on to express his intention, after a career than spans 70 years, to continue working for at least another twenty. He is still working, still photographing buildings, and as much in demand as ever. Many of his early photos are now in museums and private collections around the world.

I open the program I am holding and glance down to discover an adorable black and white photo of a naked Shulman, age 15, sitting like a bathtub baby in the pool of water he recalls so fondly. A shock of brown hair hangs over his forehead, an artful reflection of his distinctly Jazz Age haircut, and his big smile and long handsome face tilt up toward the observer. Water ripples around his knees and toes, a large boulder rests behind his head, and you can almost hear the nearby waterfalls cascading over the mountains of the Indian Canyon and down into the pools.

Almost 80 years later Shulman now stands at the podium, braced by his cane and reading a short set of remarks which express his love of Palm Springs and architecture. Julius Shulman is America's pre-eminent architectural photographer, one who made his reputation photographing the work of great modernist architects like Richard Neutra, Rudolph Shindler, Pierre Koenig, and Albert Frey. One of his most famous images is a twilight time-exposure of the Kaufman House, one of only two surviving private residences in Palm Springs designed by

Richard Neutra. The Shulman archives are now owned by the Getty Museum in Los Angeles.

When it is time for the unveiling of Shulman's star the master of ceremonies ushers Shulman over to the large red leather cushion on the sidewalk where honorees kneel to be photographed with their star. Unfortunately kneeling is no longer an option for Shulman, so one of the small white folding chairs is moved into position and the red cushion is removed. Shulman sits down with his cane and the square plywood cover is lifted to reveal Shulman's star. The accompanying brass letters read: "Julius Shulman Architectural Photographer."

I am grateful I wore my big Jackie O. sunglasses because tears fall uncontrollably from my eyes and roll down my cheeks. Julius Shulman spent his entire career as a photographer in the service of others. He dedicated himself to helping architects realize their vision in a photograph. It is work that requires talent, sensitivity, and a sophisticated understanding of design. But there isn't a lot of glamour in this work nor is it work that held the promise of fame or fortune.

I cry easily but not often, and the things that open my personal spigot of emotion are unpredictable. On at least a few occasions I have walked into buildings and been so overwhelmed by the artistry of the design and its spiritual impact that tears immediately came to my eyes. Buildings that generate this kind of response from me include the Pantheon in Rome, the Guggenheim Museums in Manhattan and Bilbao, and the Garnier Opera House in Paris.

One of the great failures of modern architecture is the inability of the profession to educate the public. Even today most Americans can barely spell architecture, much less appreciate it. Architecture simply doesn't appear on our life screens unless it is monumental in scale and prominently sited. Julius Shulman spent most of his life photographing small commercial buildings and private residences designed by visionary modernist architects whose work was unappreciated by most people. In most cases, this remains true today. But Palm Springs, with it relatively large repository of modernist buildings and a new-found respect for modern design, is now at the forefront of a modernist revival.

Despite several beautiful books by Shulman and countless others that feature his work, Shulman remains largely unknown. In a world of fame ruled by the likes of Paris Hilton, Julius Shulman is not even on the map. But here in Palm Springs, on a perfectly spectacular day, his name is now on the sidewalk – and it will remain there for the foreseeable future.

I am unexpectedly filled with an overwhelming sense of civic pride for his well-deserved recognition. And at the same time, I despair. If this sort of thing continues, will I soon be applauding wildly for Michael Flatley's *Lord of the Dance* without a trace of irony, and seriously entertaining early bird specials as valid dining opportunities?

POSTCARD
(1963)

I am thirteen. Junior high school is the lowest point of my life. I am bullied daily by male peers for being a sissy. My private pastimes outside of school are reading, riding my bicycle, and making model cars, although the latter hobby is beginning to lose its fascination.

I bring home straight A's on my report cards but nine years of private tap dance lessons provide me with my only opportunity to shine in a group activity. I have loved dancing since I took my first class at the age of five. The classes were my mother's idea. She didn't want her son growing up as a wallflower, unable to take a woman to a dance.

I am studying at my third dance studio when my instructor, like others before her, calls my mother into her office at the studio for a conference to communicate familiar information.

"Robert is an extremely gifted dancer and I have taught him everything I can. It's time for him to move on to another teacher who can give him the professional training his talent merits. There are a couple of instructors in Detroit I can recommend."

I am used to changing instructors for this reason, and the prospect of a new challenge is exciting. Tap dancing is precise, rigorous, and more fun than anything I know. My mother drives me home from my final day in class with the names, addresses, and telephone numbers of recommended instructors in her purse.

The next afternoon while my father is at work, my mother informs me my dance classes are over. There will be no new instructor and no new school. I don't understand why I'm being punished.

"Your father," she begins with a sigh of resignation, "thinks you're too old for dance class."

"Too old?"

"He thinks now that you're a teenager you should be doing other things. You should be doing the things most boys do. Dancing…..well, he just doesn't think that's the kind of thing a boy should be doing."

I am too young to get a job and pay for classes myself. And I know when a decision is final in our household.

-6-

My Next Trick: A Major Motion Picture

The message on my answering machine orders me to report to the Morongo Casino in Cabazon for the upcoming Nicolas Cage/Julianne Moore film, *Next*, directed by an alleged cross-dresser who probably knows at least as much about fellatio as I do. How can I say "no"?

Twenty years ago Cabazon, California was a dust bowl adjacent to Interstate 10, about 15 miles northwest of Palm Springs. Its landmarks were two life-sized stucco dinosaurs flanking a filling station and Hadley's Orchards, a mammoth fruit and nut emporium. The Morongo Band of Cahuilla Indians lived on a reservation nearby. Then came the wildly successful Cabazon Outlet Mall where The Gap and food courts mingle successfully with high-end retailers like Armani, Prada, and Coach.

The final nail in Cabazon's coffin of anonymity was the $250 million high rise Morongo Casino completed in 2005. Like all Indian casinos it doesn't exactly attract the social register. On an episode of the Showtime series *Huff*, Blythe Danner's character announces she is going to

Cabazon with her girlfriends to gamble. She informs her daughter-in-law that the casino is more upscale than before. By way of clarification, she adds, "Some of the gamblers actually have teeth now." For better or worse, Cabazon has arrived.

Today Hollywood goes Cabazon for one day of pick-up shots inside the casino, which is doubling for Mandalay Bay in Las Vegas. I'm asked by the woman on the telephone to dress "upscale, as if you were going on a date." Upscale seems to be the mantra for casting agents working Palm Springs location shoots. I can only assume they fear of a roomful of toothless crones will show up in sweatpants.

Next, a big-budget Hollywood action film is based on a Philip K. Dick short story about a Vegas lounge act magician (Cage) who can see into the future. He's trying to avoid capture by a government agent (Julianne Moore in the role typically played by Jodie Foster) who wants to use his special talents to prevent a terrorist attack. Cage's love interest is played by Jessica Biel. Pyrotechnics of every variety are guaranteed.

Cage can do wonders with crap material but my gut says this turkey is heading for the summer release basement. I remember *Captain Corelli's Mandolin* and *Windtalkers*. A few years ago fellow brat-packer Sean Penn declared Cage was "no longer an actor" because of his sellout to mainstream Hollywood blockbusters. He said Cage had become "more like a performer," leaving an unmistakable connotation of a trained monkey doing tricks for coins – big ones. Although Penn's assessment may seem a bit harsh it's not entirely off the mark.

Cage is talented enough to make a picture work from start to finish on its own terms. But his name above the title will not guarantee big grosses on that all-important opening weekend. One might argue that Cage sullied his own reputation after winning the Oscar by taking projects that were not only beneath his talent but, in some cases, beneath contempt. But those mainstream Hollywood summer movies come with multi-million dollar salaries. Any actor can get cast in a small indie film where he works for scale or less. The opportunity to headline a big-budget action film comes to only a few people and the opportunity doesn't last a lifetime. And like everyone else involved, I'm certainly going to cash my check. This shoot pays extras $75 for 8 hours work, with time-and-a-half for overtime - 38% more than the Kevin Williamson shoot. Food and salary costs for extras alone on this one-day shoot will easily exceed $30,000.

With specific instructions to park in the open and not in the shaded parking structure reserved for gamblers,

I pull into a space behind the casino. At least the lot is paved, unlike the dustbowl behind Parker. But the weather has turned from unseasonably cold to hot and the prediction for today is a high of 90 degrees. I pull out my sun deflector and spread it across the dashboard to keep my car as cool as possible. These things don't work perfectly but at least when I return to the car I'll be able to drive without an oven mitt.

I walk through the jangling casino to an air conditioned second floor conference room that serves as ground zero for extras. The differences between this production and the Kevin Williamson pilot are immediately apparent. The casino conference room has 14-foot ceilings, comfortable chairs, and tablecloths. The large room will easily hold all 150 background players and banquet tables are loaded with coffee (decaffeinated and regular), condiments, water, and iced tea. Melissa, a pretty blond seated at the front table, asks for my name, checks me off her list, and hands me my payment voucher.

As I'm filling out the voucher I ask Melissa, "So tell me, did they give Nick Cage a good wig this time out?"

Melissa looks up at me as if I'd just asked if she were still sexually abusing her children. My question goes unanswered as I back away from the table with my completed voucher.

Each day you work you receive a new voucher. There are spaces on the voucher identifying the name of the project and the production company, as well as blocks for the time you report to work, the time you leave, and the precise times you are dismissed to eat lunch, which is always complementary. There are also blanks for assigned props and wardrobe control (if wardrobe provides you with a costume, they keep your payment voucher and don't return it until the costume comes back). At the end of the day one of the people in charge reviews and signs-off on each voucher. Then it is sent with all the other vouchers to a payroll service that cuts and mails the check, deducting the appropriate amounts for income taxes and social security. They pay promptly.

This is a big-budget production. Melissa and her cohort Sable, an assistant director, are casually dressed but they have expensive haircuts and a personal acquaintance with cosmetic dentistry. I spot a few folks who also worked on the Kevin Williamson project with me, but I elect to sit apart from them. A pretty, buxom girl sits down at my table and we strike up a conversation. She has two small children and she pulls out her cell phone to show me a picture of her youngest, a chubby-cheeked ten-month-old boy. A sister who lives nearby is at home watching the kids, and her husband is on duty at the Twenty-nine Palms Marine base.

"I grew up as an Army brat," she volunteers. "I guess I got used to that life when I was little, so when I married a Marine it didn't bother me moving around the country all the time. When we lived in Austin, Texas, I had an agent."

"Did the agent get you much work?"

"Some. And I got some on my own."

"Did your agent take a percentage of the work you got on your own?"

"No. But every time I got a job without her she made me feel like some sort of criminal or something – like, a traitor. But I mean, I needed the work and she wasn't getting me enough. I did a few commercials and a rock video in Austin."

"You know who you look like?"

"No."

"You look like a combination of Marilyn McCoo and Jennifer Beals."

A sweet but noticeably blank smile appears on her face.

"You've never heard of them, have you?"

"No," she shrugs.

"Marilyn was one of the lead singers in *The Fifth Dimension* and Jennifer Beals starred in *Flashdance*. She's on Showtime's *The L Word* right now."

"I'll have to look out for them."

"How old are you?"

"I'm 26."

"Never mind."

After all the extras are checked-in we're sent to wardrobe. The wardrobe department is in the adjoining conference room only a few steps away. There are tables and racks full of clothes behind the wardrobe mistress who leans against one of the front tables, assessing her subjects one by one. I immediately miss the sweet-natured costumer from the Kevin Williamson project because this woman is strictly Cruella deVille. A thin brown-haired devil of indeterminate middle-age, she no doubt wears Prada while vacationing in her native Rhineland. I survive her cursory inspection without a problem but my new friend from 29 Palms is given a low-cut print dress that accentuates her two most visible assets. Back in the holding area the extras all remark about the brusque, unpleasant demeanor of the wardrobe mistress.

Once everyone returns from wardrobe the room is full of generic gamblers, uniformed security guards, cashiers in brocade vests, black-suited government agents, and a trio of rhinestone cowgirls. Melissa stands at the front of the room and asks for our attention.

"I want to welcome all the newcomers, and welcome back those of you who are returning from the last time we were here. I hope you all have fun today. We're shooting one scene and it will probably be a long day. In a few hours, we'll be bringing you a snack and we should break for lunch around noon. I don't know if they'll be setting up banquet tables in the hall or if you'll be allowed to eat at the casino's buffet. I'll find out and let you know. In the meantime you need to stay in this room at all times when you're not on the set. There are bathrooms just outside at either end of the hall. If you need to have a cigarette you can go down to the casino floor and smoke near the bottom of the escalator. Smoking is permitted in the casino but don't hang around in groups and block access to the escalator. That's about all for now. One of the assistant directors will be coming up soon and bringing people down to the set."

Right on cue a petite young woman in jeans comes through the door and into the holding room. She speaks without introducing herself.

"Okay. I'm going to start taking people down to the set now. Oh….hold on. They're talking to me."

She stops and listens to the instructions coming to her though her earpiece.

"Copy that," she replies into her tiny hand-held microphone, then turns back to the room and picks up where she left off.

"Alright now. If I don't pick you, please don't take it personally. It doesn't mean I don't like you. We just try to get a good mix of ages and types. If I don't pick you for this set-up, that doesn't mean I won't need you later."

With that she goes around the room, selecting about 25 people and leading them downstairs. By 11 a.m. less than half the extras have been called and I am not among them. The rest of us remain munching in air-conditioned comfort on our morning snack: chicken or vegetarian pita bread sandwiches, in an unlimited supply, selected from large bowls set up at the back of the room.

While I wait to be called I read a book I'm assigned to review for the *Bay Area Reporter*. One of the gray-haired bouffants at my table, who lives in a trailer park in Cathedral City, inquires about my diligence.

"That book must be really good. You hardly look up."

"Actually, it is pretty good. But I'm also working. I'm a book reviewer and this is an assignment."

"Oh my gosh," she exclaims. "You're double dipping! You're getting paid to be an extra and you're getting paid to read."

"Yes, that's true."

I decide it would serve no useful purpose to point out that the combined income from my concurrent glamorous endeavors hardly constitutes a living wage. Some illusions are best left in place.

We break for lunch and are given vouchers entitling us to the abundanza of the casino's enormous buffet. At 2 p.m. I'm finally sent down to the set. Two extras I know from the Kevin Williamson project are called at the same time and we all meet at the escalator. One of them is a distinguished looking guy in a gray suit who always looks like he just walked off stage from playing Don Quixote in *Man of La Mancha*. The other is a woman of about fifty who could be Heather Locklear's older sister. She is immaculately groomed and perfectly dressed, with her bodacious ta-tas prominently displayed. The elder Locklear inserts herself between Don Quixote and me, wrapping her arms through ours and marching us toward the set like the Three Geritol Musketeers.

"Come on boys," she cheers. "Let's go get 'em."

"At least this day is going to be easier than that Kevin Williamson shoot," I reply.

"Oh, honey that one just about killed me. I got a terrible cold after we walked up and down Palm Canyon all night. I just about froze to death."

"I know. And I worked the next night at Parker, outside in the rain."

"I was supposed to," she adds. "But I didn't show up. There's no way I could have done that a second night. I was home in bed under the covers."

Don Quixote, who also worked both nights with me on the Kevin Williamson shoot, changes the subject as we pass the high speed elevators that take diners up 27 floors to the restaurant and disco on top of the casino.

"Have you been up there for dinner?" he asks, nodding in the direction of the elevators.

"No. I thought about it because the view must be sensational. With the local building codes the only high rises in the valley are the Indian casinos."

"Yeah, I thought the same thing about the view so I went for dinner. When I got there I discovered all the booths in the restaurant face into the room instead of out at the view."

"Are you shitting me?"

"No. I couldn't believe it."

As we approach the set the elder Locklear looks down at her gold lace and spandex shell and turns to me, "Do you think I'm showing too much cleavage?"

Before I can reply she meows, "Oh, but that wouldn't interest you, would it?"

"No, you skanky bitch. I wouldn't suck on those things if I was suffocating and they were filled with oxygen." That's what I think of saying but I remain silent. It's going to be a long shoot and it just isn't worth going there.

When we arrive at the set Sable directs us to wait in one corner while she gets instructions from the director for the first set-up. She returns and explains the basics to the extras before giving us our placements and movement. Nicolas Cage's character walks up to the cashier's window to redeem his chips. A psycho gunman comes up and attempts a hold up. The gunman shoots a security guard.

At least two dozen crew members, three productions assistants, the make-up woman with her really bad facelift, and all the extras are crowded into one corner of the casino where a fake cashier's window has been constructed. The entire space used for the shoot is no more than 900 square feet so we are all close together. Cables and sophisticated monitors are everywhere and although we are almost falling over each other, everyone is respectful of each other's space and clear about their assignments.

Two large 35 millimeter Panavision cameras also allow for shooting the scene in videotape first before film rolls, allowing the director to preview the shots on the video monitor and decide if the composition and camera movement approximate what he desires.

We rehearse the first shot with the stand-ins. Each extra must remember where he is in the scene when the action and dialogue unfold so shots can be matched and background players can place themselves appropriately even if only a section of the scene is being reshot.

"Drop that gun" is the line shouted over and over for the next four hours, followed by the screams of the actress playing the cashier. I walk the same 20-foot path for the duration. But this task is made considerably more interesting due to the presence of director Lee Tamahori.

From my point of view the real draw for this one night stand is Tamahori. He has several projects in development right now but I wouldn't be surprised if they evaporate before he gets a chance to step behind the camera. It hasn't been a good year for Tamahori. This may be reflected in websites like "Hollywood .com" that list his profession as "director, boom operator."

Tamahori, a native of New Zealand, was born to a Maori father and British mother. He started crewing on Kiwi productions in the '80s and had a great international success in 1994 as director of *Once Were Warriors*, a tale of Maori domestic abuse that parallels the decline of New Zealand's indigenous tribes. After that Tamahori secured regular mainstream directing work, helming the 2002 James Bond flick, *Die Another Day* as well as 2005's *XXX: State of the Union*. Tamahori and I are both the same age and gay. But for Tamahori the offal hit the oscillator just a few months before principal photography began on *Next*, when he was busted on Santa Monica Boulevard.

Tamahori reportedly offered an undercover Los Angeles police officer a blow job for money. That, in Hollywood, is something you might sweep under the table by ignoring it to death, especially if your face isn't known to millions. But at the time the alleged offer was made Tamahori was reportedly wearing a black wig and off-the-shoulder dress. The director/boom operator/drag queen was charged with solicitation and loitering and released on $2,000 bail. He retained Scott Peterson's attorney, Mark Geragos, but before he was to appear in court for arraignment Tamahori wisely copped a plea of "no contest" to misdemeanor criminal trespassing and settled for 3 years of probation, 15 days of community service with the Hollywood Beautification Project (making sure shoes and bags match?), and a $390 fine.

The notoriously heterosexual and frequently homophobic money men in Hollywood do not take this sort of thing lightly. Not since George Michael worked that tea room or Hugh Grant picked up Divine Brown has there been such a case of bad judgment on the streets of Los Angeles. I'm sure Tamahori's contractual ink for *Next* was already dry at the time of the incident. But for the sake of his career, Next better be a blockbuster.

The usual collection of testosterone poisoned male heterosexual crew members gather around the diminutive Tamahori who is short and slight of frame, with a thin, bird-like upper torso and Eurasian look. He wears a white t-shirt over gray sweatpants and sports a three-day growth of white stubble below short-cropped white hair.

Tamahori moves with a strange mixture of certainty and confusion as he sets up the shot and rehearses with stand-ins and extras. He is clearly the man in charge but most of the instructions come from assistant directors. I find it impossible not to imagine him sashaying down Santa Monica Boulevard in that wig and off-the-shoulder dress, doing his personal impression of "Hey, sailor." It takes all of my self-control to suppress inappropriate laughter.

After the shot is choreographed, one of the assistant directors calls to a production assistant, "Okay. Please invite Nick to come to the set now." I find this instruction fascinating.

First of all, the director does not call for the actor personally. And despite the host of wireless earpieces and microphones that facilitate crew communication throughout the casino, none is connected to the star. Most importantly there is no "Where's Nick?" or "Go get Nick." Instead the third party request for the star is extended in the form of "please invite." I wish these guys worked in my house around dinner time when I was a kid.

Nicolas Cage arrives in a costume similar to that worn by his younger and more handsome stand-in. He is much transformed from the guy I used to see occasionally in San Francisco. A decade ago he had a few wispy strands of brown hair pushed back from his shrinking widow's peak. But Cage now sports a fuller widow's peak, one that appears to have been filled-in by extensive hair transplants. It's good work and worth whatever it cost. The hair is pushed back and curiously full at the sides and back of his head, suggesting a supplemental hair weave or extensions.

At 42, Cage has about 8 years left as a viable leading man in Hollywood films, and although some bald men can be incredibly sexy, Cage is not among them. He does not possess the buff, youthful demeanor of Vin Diesel, nor does he have the spectacular beauty of the older Ed Harris. In Cage's case, hair transplants were a good career move. His teeth have been capped to replace the rodent-like pegs on display 1986's, *The Boy in Blue*, and his face is covered with pancake makeup. Cage's costume is a rumpled black tuxedo and green ruffled shirt, with no tie and black pointed-toe, ankle-high boots. The overall vision would recall Halloween if you saw him on the street, but it will play fine on the big screen.

I end up standing near him for the rest of the shoot. Cage is 5'9" tall and reed thin. He has delicate hands, the kind you see on Lladro porcelain figurines, with short fingers that taper toward the fingernails. His face is striking because of its unusual composition. The hooked nose does not look particularly Italian, despite the fact that he was born Nicolas Coppola, and his jaw line heads immediately south from the bottom of relatively small ears. His large brown eyes convey an intensity that is never broken by a smile but he does not seem taciturn.

By all accounts Cage is a nice guy. His demeanor today fluctuates between serious and seriously bored since most of his time on set is spent waiting. He makes frequent calls on a borrowed cell phone and at one point, Cage calls out, "Where's Hans?"

A stocky, middle-aged blond assistant walks over to Cage when he hears his name.

"Call Oliver Stone back and see if we can set up something for Friday."

Hans nods and walks away without comment.

As the afternoon progresses the shoot becomes complicated because it must be captured in many similar, but not identical ways. The scene is shot as it would unfold if Cage's character could not see into the future and the security guard is killed in the robbery. It is also shot as it would unfold if Cage's character acts on his ability to see the future and stops the robbery before it can take place. And finally one take is a freeze-frame on Cage to allow for the insertion of a digital sequence in which Cage's character envisions the future. Each of these shots involves different placement of extras and repeated takes.

After one of the takes, Tamahori yells "cut" and I turn to a friendly, tall extra placed behind me. He wears a maroon sport coat and his long brown hair is woven into a braid that hangs down the middle of his back.

"Are you an American Indian?"

"Yeah," he nods.

"You're not a member of the Cahuilla tribe, are you?"

"No way. I'm one-quarter Apache. You don't think I'd be doing this if I was a Cahuilla Indian, do you?"

We both laugh at the preposterous idea that millionaire Casino owners would be working as extras. An assistant director calls out, "Background, quietly reset to one." This is the last take and at 6:45 p.m., a little more than 12 hours after I reported, I'm released.

-7-

Dancer from the Dance

April is Palm Springs' unofficial gay month, beginning with The Dinah Shore for lesbians. The Dinah is to lesbians what Capistrano is to swallows. Thousands of women pour into Palm Springs, filling all the downtown hotels, to dance, sunbathe, and hang out at a variety of parties. The festivities coincide with the Kraft/Nabisco Championship LPGA golf tournament, formerly known as The Dinah Shore Invitational. This year the parties are occurring under the shadow of litigation.

A consortium of three women is responsible for what is now known in lesbian circles as "The Dinah Shore Weekend." They are the women who first organized and promoted this special event for lesbians. There was a schism after last year's event and one of women, Mariah Hanson, sued the other women, life-partners Sandy Sachs and Robin Gans. Her suit filed in United States District Court in San Francisco alleges her former partners have disparaged her reputation and hindered her ability to make a living by failing to disclose some ticket sales and customer lists to her.

As the lawsuits fly the lesbian parties continue in separate venues under separate names. Hopefully the founders will realize there are enough interested participants to accommodate expanded offerings under two different banners. But there is big money in these events, and whenever big money is at stake conflict is rarely far behind.

The White Party follows The Dinah Shore a week or two later on Easter weekend. Larger in size than the women's event, White Party's headliners this year are Toni Braxton and Australian disco diva Anastacia. Since my taste for dancing all night ended sometime around the time they closed the I-Beam on Haight Street, I am not attending. Frankly, I feel this sort of partying is no longer age appropriate for me, even if I were able to summon the energy and enthusiasm I once brought to the task.

In the 1980s I made up my own circuit parties before there was such a thing as a circuit, working my way onto the dance floor at Heaven in London, The Palace in Paris, The Saint in Manhattan, and the Giftcenter and Galeria Center parties in San Francisco. They were fun. That was then; this is now.

Sitting in my living room on Sunday evening, the last night of White Party, I hear the fireworks going off, marking the end of the celebration. Thanks to my years in San Francisco I'm an expert at hearing fireworks. Every year San Francisco puts on a six-figure fireworks display over the bay for the Fourth of July. Unfortunately July is one of the foggiest months and before the fireworks can begin a thick blanket of fog always rolls in making it impossible to see anything. But you can hear the popping as invisible projectiles soar skyward from their distant launch point.

This is what I hear tonight at 9 p.m. I walk outside and stand in my nightshirt in the driveway of my home. Little Bill saunters out to stand by my side. This time I can actually see the fireworks splashing bursts of color against the black desert sky. The strains of Donna Summer's "Last Dance" float on the ether over Warm Sands and I grow unexpectedly nostalgic for those party days in the era of Levi's 501's and Lacoste shirts. I hope the guys shaking their booties under the Palm Springs party tent are having at least as much fun as I had in what now seems like a past life.

The next day I pick up my latest book review assignment, the paperback release of Joshua Gamson's biography of Sylvester entitled *The Fabulous Sylvester*.

Gamson is a PhD sociologist and scrupulous researcher. And unlike most academics, he can actually write. Perusing the footnotes in the back of the book I discover the 1988 interview I did with Sylvester shortly before his death is included as part of the source material for Gamson's biography. The same interview, published originally in the *San Francisco Sentinel*, was previously excerpted in the book *Tribal Rites* by David Diebold.

Sylvester was a San Francisco character of amazing talent and individuality who went straight to the top of the disco heap at the peak of the international disco craze. But as soon as he arrived at the pinnacle of the recording industry the disco phenomenon began to collapse. A gay, black man with a flair for makeup, dresses, and outrageous behavior both on and off stage, Sylvester used his falsetto voice to infuse a gospel sound into dance music. Yet when we met that day in 1988, the performer I once knew was no longer visible.

His condo at 80 Collingwood Street was just a block from where I lived on the corner of Castro and Market Streets. And when his personal attendant left and Sylvester emerged from his bedroom to join me in the living room, I was stunned by his visible deterioration. His glossy jet black skin had turned ashen and his formerly flawless complexion was littered with tiny bumps.

Sylvester had lost at least 50 pounds. His hair was pulled back in a small bun and house slippers covered his feet. I knew immediately I could not write about any of these things because Sylvester would read them and the printed description of his physical decline could only make him depressed.

I gave him a hug and determined my most important and immediate task was to lift his spirits. It wasn't easy. But as my genuine enthusiasm for him and his work became apparent some of the old spark returned to his voice. The instrumental portion of what would be his next studio album was already complete but he was too sick to record the vocals. His one attempt resulted in an unusable track marred by coughing and shortness of breath.

"I just can't seem to get my chops," he complained.

Too Hot to Sleep, a sultry collection of ballads was Sylvester's final album for Fantasy Records before he moved over to Megatone.

"That's my favorite album of yours. I still play it all the time."

"Oh. Well, it's not one of my favorites."

"What was up with that cover? Is sort of looked like some Georgia O'Keefe painting of the southwest."

"That's the only album I made that didn't have my picture on the cover. They (Fantasy) wanted to change my image, but I said, 'You're not changing me. As a matter of fact, I'll show you.'

"I put on this big drag queen purple negligee, a wig and some makeup, and I was standing around in the lobby of the record company in broad daylight. I sashayed into the elevator to the president's office and I swirled around in front of him and said, 'You may be trying to change my image but I'm not. This is the image.' So they put me on suspension. No one in recording history at that time had been as outrageous as I was, and I think they were afraid of me. I was rebellious I'm sure, and awful. But I was intending to be."

That was Sylvester. I did that interview because I wanted to give him some form of recognition for the joy his music brought into my life. Within a few years of Sylvester's death his manager Tim McKenna and my friend and editor at the *San Francisco Sentinel*, Eric Hellman, were also dead from AIDS.

While I'm still thumbing through my review copy of *The Fabulous Sylvester*, Little Bill paws at my leg reminding me it's time for his late afternoon walk. As we turn the corner onto Camino Parocela in front of Bacchanal, I hear music coming over the walls of the resort. It is Sylvester singing "Mighty Real," the song title I borrowed for the headline of my 1988 interview. The coincidence is so startling it instantly gives rise to goose bumps and causes the hair on my forearms to stand at attention.

Vietnam was the war of my generation. AIDS is the holocaust of my peers. Although it continues to devastate the population of the world, in 1981 it arrived as an uninvited guest and took up residence in homes from which it could not be expelled. I ultimately became somewhat comfortable talking about it in critiques of books, films, and art. The heartbreaking documentary *Silverlake Diary*, the compassionate and wise film *Longtime Companion*, and the Pulitzer Prize-winning *Angels in America* are part of our national artistic legacy from the horrible years.

In 1984 I was an author and original cast member in a play called *The A.I.D.S Show: Artists Involved in Death and Survival.* It was a workshop production involving a group of San Francisco writers and actors who came together at Theater Rhinoceros to create a play that would address the national nightmare unfolding in our community. Our goal was to validate and explore our shared experience and to help heal our sorrow. Our show was the first play produced in America on the subject of

AIDS. It was a grueling, cathartic, and rewarding endeavor that ultimately toured the country and became the subject of a PBS documentary. After I left the cast of *The A.I.D.S. Show* I stopped reading and writing about the health crisis because I needed to protect my psyche from the groundswell of bad news. There was no hope on the horizon; the future held only an endless series of memorial services.

Yet all the loss and pain I stifled and shoved down for so long left a permanent lump in my throat. My friends in San Francisco began dying in large numbers in 1982. President Reagan did not even mention the word AIDS until February, 1986. Almost four years passed and thousands of Americans died before the President of the United States would even mention the word AIDS. As far as I'm concerned this is the legacy of the Reagan years. Recent events only enhance my still simmering sense of outrage.

We now face the possibility of an avian flu epidemic that may arise sometime in the future. Keep in mind it has not materialized and for the few cases already diagnosed in Europe and Asia the mortality rate is low. Yet the Internet, the nightly news, and presidential proclamations are full of information about what the

United States is doing to prepare for the possibility of such an epidemic – one that may not even arrive.

Different departments of Federal, State and local government are holding meetings and earmarking funds to address potential problems. Meanwhile health care professionals are trying to come up with a vaccine. But in the 1980s the United States stuck its head in the sand while my friends died, in much the same way the international community continues to turn its back on the problem of AIDS in Africa. In America in the early 1980s, it looked like AIDS was just going to wipe out queers. In Africa now, it's just those impoverished black people. Neither group controls any of the world's fossil fuel reserves; we were - and they are - to a large extent perceived as expendable.

I have kept my distance from the subject for a long time. It's a downer. It is personal. It still cannot be fixed. But beneath all my observations AIDS remains the subject that will continue to inform the rest of my life. It is a deep, dark, poisoned well from which I cannot allow myself to drink. Therein lies madness.

POSTCARD

(1966-1968)

I am sixteen. Armed with my learner's permit, my father takes me on a Sunday outing to monitor my driving skills. Our house is on East Outer Drive and the street is divided into two lanes of one-way traffic on each side, separated by a large center median and nicely landscaped with colorful plants that bloom from spring until fall. It is a beautiful residential street, lined with Dutch Elms, and a good training ground for student drivers.

I pilot the Oldsmobile with relative ease despite its bulk. My father and I are in one of our periods of détente. These episodes frequently coincide with his vacations. When freed from the tedium of his work at the Uniroyal factory on Jefferson Avenue my father likes to go fishing on the St. Clair River. I like to see him go.

The light ahead turns red and I bring the car to a stop just before the crosswalk on Harper. Still looking straight ahead, my father asks, "So whaddya want to do when you grow up?"

"I don't know. Dad I'm only in tenth grade."

"I guess you're right. You got lots of time to make up your mind."

"What did you want to do when you were my age?"

"I didn't have a lot of choices. You gotta remember things back then weren't like they are now. Times were tough."

"Why did you drop out of high school?"

"I wasn't a good student. There didn't seem to be much point to staying in school." The light changes green. "Put on your turn signal and turn right. We'll go down Harper to Chalmers, then circle back to Outer Drive."

I execute his command.

"But did you ever think you'd spend twenty years working in a factory?"

"I took what I could get. The work's hard, but the money is good."

I decide to push the normal bounds of our superficial exchanges and go deeper.

"But what was important to you in life? What was the thing you most wanted for yourself?"

My father actually takes a moment to ponder this question before he responds.

"I always wanted to be a regular guy."

My eyes and ears remain focused on the road but my mind reels from the simplicity of his revelation and its bearing on our relationship.

"You mean you wanted to be like everyone else? You wanted to be a regular Joe, one of the gang?"

"Yeah. Doesn't everybody?"

Pulling my father's car back onto Outer Drive I understand it would be best to leave his assumption unchallenged. But in doing so I would tacitly invalidate my own choices. I decide to lob one last ball over the net.

"I never wanted to be a regular guy and I never will. It doesn't interest me. I guess I need more of a challenge."

Silence settles in before our conversation returns to mirrors, turn signals, and crosswalks. A week later I pass my driver's test and get my license. A year later I am named valedictorian of my high school class and receive a certificate in the mail that contains my name and the honor bestowed on me. My father buys a small frame for the certificate and places it on the dresser in his bedroom where it will remain until his death.

———

-8-

Ten Cents a Prance

Helios is a small clothing-optional resort for men on the north end of Palm Springs. Formerly operating as a gay resort under the name La Posada, it remains one of those white stucco, red tile roof venues that began life decades earlier as a weekend retreat for straight people. Now reinvented once again by a ménage a trios of business partners, the new Helios is hosting the first rentboy.com pool party since 2004. Rentboy.com is an international, online compendium of 'ho-to-go specialists who make themselves available to guys who sometimes prefer takeout to the standard home-cooked affair. The cock tale of Helios and this particular website seems like a perfect party marriage.

But at the 2 p.m. start time none of the fillies can be found at the starting gate. The scheduled 12-2 p.m. "V.I.P." meat and greet didn't happen; the bar has no liquor; the resort provides no towels; and even with a meager crowd of early arrivals there isn't enough room in the resort for everyone to sit in the sun. The three partners who run the resort scurry around naked carrying walky-talkies and proudly sporting matching Prince Alberts. Tom Weise, the owner of rentboy.com, also flits about in a nice-fitting spandex bathing suit that flatters his lean, muscular body.

The deadly calm of early afternoon is interrupted only by the change of shift on the swimming pool's one pool float. A splashy dismount by one rider is always followed by a quiet respectful period in which the float does what floats are supposed to do and slowly bumps off the tiled edges of the pool. Within minutes a different poolside guest will decide a polite amount of time has passed. Leaving a towel draped across his chaise like the "reserved" sign on a restaurant table, he will jump into the pool and pounce on the float, taking temporary possession.

I pause my stroll though the crowd and sit in a plastic chair beneath the shaded overhang of the resort's western wing. Immediately in front of me at one of the glass-topped patio tables, a different drama unfolds in pantomime. One barefoot young man in a pair of surfing trunks has been in the same seat since my arrival, crying softly but continuously. His tear-stained face recalls a contemporary gay incarnation of Picasso's famous weeping woman, Dora Maar.

Clearly a victim of love gone wrong, Mr. Maar is inconsolable. Just out of earshot I measure the extent of his emotional devastation by watching the failure of friends who stop, one by one, to take up temporary residence beside his chair. Three different men try to offer assistance or consolation and their ministrations miraculously coincide with the revolving availability of the pool float. An arm embraces his shoulder, hands stroke his forearms, and heads lean compassionately in his direction to whisper words of encouragement, all to no avail. The slow trickle of tears continues unabated as his friends surrender to an impenetrable wall of grief that will not be breached. Just beyond his subculture of isolation the party goes on.

As rent boys and porn models gradually emerge the deejay goes to work and patrons start arriving. Soon the bar, now stocked with liquor, is hopping. The junk food buffet attracts some attention but most eyes are focused on the hot guys in the micro spandex suits. Yet the rent boys ignore paying guests who could be their best customers and persist in celebrating their own fabulousness by hanging together in little groups and smoking cigarettes. They preen and prance around the grounds like the prettiest girls at a junior high school dance and, for the first time, I fully appreciate why "It's Hard Out Here for a Pimp" deserved that Oscar.

But around 6 p.m. when the sun goes behind the mountains and the light falters, the action begins in earnest. A trio of porn models begins a seemingly impromptu demonstration of their talents in the large Jacuzzi. The naked action is strictly oral and will continue for over an hour as new couplings begin and old ones end. But the bacchanalian potential of the event doesn't quite spill over into the general crowd, partially because the resort, whose outdoor sling remains empty all evening, does not have many darkened nooks and crannies that encourage ribaldry.

The guy standing next to me just outside the Jacuzzi area turns and asks a rhetorical question, "Could this be any less erotic?"

"I know what you mean," I reply. "The flashbulbs don't help."

The Jacuzzi's low wall is surrounded by overweight middle-aged men holding cameras, obsessively capturing the hot tub action on film as if it were the red carpet on Oscar night. Reasoning deductively, it is probably safe to assume this is the closest they will ever get to this sort of coupling without writing a much bigger check than the $30 price of admission. Nearby in one of the resort's rooms, a couple of boys leave the blinds open so a gaggle of voyeurs can observe their coupling.

At 8:30 p.m. the excruciatingly annoying Angel Benton takes the microphone and, in his helium-inspired voice, emcees a talent show and charity auction that effectively kills the party. Porn models auction off their underwear and bathing suits, mostly to each other. An increasingly disappointed crowd is not in a philanthropic mood. A lucky V.I.P. patron wins the drawing for a one-hour private session with the very hot Tony Dancer and a talent-free vocalist named Shiko Aviance (who actually brought a woman with him to this event) does high kicks before launching into his song. His performance is defeated by scratchy reverb from the sound system and a costume that features white shoes, white pants, and Aviance's naked upper torso framed by a silver lame bolero top.

One of the young escorts, a tall, dark-haired beauty in a turquoise bathing suit, sits alone in a chair just outside the resort's reception desk. His square shoulders and hairless chest arch as he slouches forward and runs long fingers through tousled curls. His legs are spread open and his pelvis thrusts forward beyond the edge of his chair. With his free hand he frequently rearranges the position of his large penis inside his suit. Although he does not display the level of despair established hours earlier by the weeping man, he is clearly on a downer. And like the weeping man he, too, is consoled by his friends.

Escorts and porn models stop to encourage him to join in the auction on stage. But these visits are shorter and more to the point than the ministrations offered the weeping man. Several men stop and grab his hand, attempting unsuccessfully to pull him up and out of the chair. One model walks over and unceremoniously kneels in front of the escort taking up a position between his knees. He wordlessly removes the man's penis from its turquoise lair and half-heartedly goes to work. But not even fellatio can dispel the escort's dour mood, much less inspire him to an erection.

I laugh quietly to myself as I recall the production assistant from the Kevin Williamson pilot who asked, "What do you do, anyway?"

Somewhere between the Jacuzzi photo shoot and the Aviance attack, I once again settle into a chair, this time in the bar area next to a sweet-faced young blond who could be a college freshman. His long-sleeved shirt and long blue jeans betray a visitor status.

"So where are you from?"

"I'm from Sonoma County," he replies.

That vagary leads rather quickly to the revelation that he is a porn model who works under the name Jessie Zane. He has only been in the business a year, but with boyish good looks and a J-Lo booty he already has six films to his credit. When I ask if he ever thinks of Joey Stefano, he looks at me as if I'm speaking Cantonese. The drug overdose of the famous gay porn bottom predates Zane's new-found career by several years.

"It won't last forever but I'm having fun," he explains. "I enjoy it. And when you're not under contract to a studio you can do as many films as you want in a short amount of time."

"How did you get started?"

"My boyfriend, Dax, got into it first and then he asked me to do a film with him."

Dax, a petite and beautifully muscled young man takes the seat on the other side of Zane and is joined by one of the rent boys who plops down in his lap and begins canoodling. Within a few minutes, Dax places his hands in the boy's shorts and pulls out his erect penis.

The evening is warm but not particularly sultry. The power of the stars against a desert sky is diminished by the jaundiced glow of a full yellow moon. In silence I muse about love's labors before kissing Jessie Zane on both cheeks, in the European style, and disappearing into the night.

-9-

The Buck Stops Here

Governor Arnold Schwarzenegger was born July 30, 1947 and his birthday is a few days away. Only a movie star governor could get me to venture beyond my swimming pool on a hot July morning and head downtown to Peabody's Café and Coffee Shop.

Peabody's occupies two storefronts on Palm Canyon next door to Enzo's, the Italian Restaurant that doubled as a coffee shop for the *Hidden Palms* television pilot. These old storefronts represent the kind of structures preservationists speak lovingly about when attempting to block the demolition of some existing building to make way for new construction that might revitalize the commercial dead zone that is now downtown Palm Springs. Change does not come easily in our town and no-growth advocates have fairly successfully driven new development down valley over the years by means of political activism, often accompanied by lawsuits.

Peabody's remains a funky down-home sort of place with ceiling fans, a concrete floor, and brick walls painted a cream color. Two rows of tables line the sidewalk outside the café. On the interior, worn teal fabric covers the beat-up wooden chairs that surround tile-topped tables. It's the kind of coffee shop you would expect to find in a college town, full of students text messaging or working on their laptops. Dozens of snapshots of famous patrons surround the entry doors and a large wall sculpture of brightly painted wooden fish impersonates art on the north wall. It is one of the few places in Palm Springs that actually recalls the little neighborhood cafes I frequented in San Francisco.

I park my car behind Peabody's in the public parking structure on Indian and walk toward Palm Canyon. On the way I saunter past two policemen who stand on the curb next to their black and white making sure no one moves the orange traffic cones that reserve the curbside parking in front of Peabody's. Although the early morning temperature is a balmy 100 degrees I reject the possibility of an outside table, no matter how shaded, in favor of air conditioned comfort inside.

The coffee shop is already jammed with breakfast patrons awaiting the governor's arrival. Schwarzenegger, who is running for re-election, is scheduled to make a campaign appearance here in one hour. There is only one African-American in an otherwise Caucasian crowd comprised of both tourists and townies. I grab the last stool at the coffee bar and order a latte. Before my drink arrives I'm approached by a smiling middle-aged woman in a pink knit halter top and white linen shorts who thrusts a large card into my hands.

A big, toothy smile beams out from beneath her brown bouffant as she asks, "Would you like to sign the governor's birthday card?"

"Oh okay," I reply, with the kind of conviction only a registered Democrat could provide.

"And how about a sticker?"

"Sure."

Her unrestrained enthusiasm brings an involuntary smile to my face.

"Why not join the party? That's what I say," she adds.

The woman peels off a green and white egg-shaped sticker containing the governor's re-election campaign slogan: "Schwarzenegger – Protecting the California Dream." She hands me the sticker and I park it on my white t-shirt. Then she hands me the governor's birthday card and a pen.

"How old is Schwarzenegger?" I ask as I prop the large birthday card on the bar in front of me.

"He turns 59 in two days."

"I see," I reply. That means he's a Leo, like me."

In clear legible handwriting I sign the card "XXOO – Ron Jeremy" before handing it back to its owner.

"Thanks," she replies with a perky lilt before heading off to gather other signatures.

In the last decade Palm Springs has become heavily Democratic in its political complexion, thanks in large part to the migration of gays and lesbians to the city. Yet the Coachella Valley remains a Republican stronghold due to the number of well-heeled voters in east valley communities like Rancho Mirage, Palm Desert, and La Quinta. Our U.S. Congresswoman is Representative Mary Bono, the Republican widow of downhill racer Sonny Bono. Our representative in Sacramento is State Congresswoman Bonnie Garcia, also a Republican. But even among Democrats, Schwarzenegger is not unpopular.

The governor has shrewdly carved out a niche for himself that sets him apart from the Bush administration and its seemingly endless series of bungled political moves. As a Hollywood actor who got his start as a competitive body builder, it should come as no surprise that although he tows the party line, Schwarzenegger is not homophobic. Despite a few missteps that include failed initiatives that took on California teachers and nurses, the governor's re-election is a certainty.

The waiter places my latte on the bar and I scan the room to survey the action. One policeman hovers by the back wall in case he's needed and reporters and photographers work the room, snapping photos and picking up quotes for local color. The café's five overhead televisions are tuned to different stations, silently telecasting picture but not sound. Peabody's waitresses, accustomed to the quiet pace of off-season, are having a meltdown trying to handle the crowd.

Behind the bar Jorge the busboy is on the phone. A blond waitress shouts instructions to him in pigeon Spanish.

"*Su hijo. Venga por favor. Rapido*," is her plea for last minute help to handle the crowd.

When Jorge truncates his telephone call the waitress realizes she has been given one double latte too many and she turns to me.

"You want it?" she asks.

"Sure."

I chug my first latte and begin working on my second, fearing I could be flying from the ceiling fan or peeing down my leg before the main event takes place. In either case I have no intention of giving up my barstool to anyone.

Every seat in the café is now is occupied and the aisles are beginning to fill with a standing-room-only crowd. Outside the sidewalk is impassable as pedestrians gather in front of Peabody's.

There is only one handsome man inside the café: a square-jawed thirtysomething blond who sports a crew cut and blue blazer and moves in and out of the crowd. Soon our chubby-cheeked State Congresswoman, Bonnie Garcia, shows up in a tank top and too-tight white pants, followed by local architect and Palm Springs City Councilman, Chris Mills. They do a little glad-handing before placing themselves conspicuously at the front of the restaurant to make sure they are the first faces the Governor sees when he enters the building.

On the television behind the bar a CNN tickertape at the bottom of the screen announces new heat-related deaths in California as the elderly and poor are forced to choose between paying the rent or having air conditioning. Choosing the former has meant death for 129 Californians already in this long, hot summer.

At 9:50 a.m. waitresses start delivering bottled water to those assembled outside on the sidewalk and standing in the sun. No politician wants to see his constituents pass out from heat stroke just as his limousine pulls up.

When I look to my right, I realize I've been joined by a bespectacled man in his fifties who wears brown suede lederhosen over a linen shirt with knee-high white socks. His female companion sports a floor-length blue dirndl skirt topped by a form-fitting red felt vest and white blouse. I recognize the homage to Schwarzenegger's native Austria but on a 100-degree plus desert morning the couple simply looks ridiculous. I make a silent vow to punch their lights out if they break into a chorus of "Edelweiss."

At 10:30a.m. - a half-hour after the governor's scheduled arrival time - the handsome blond emerges once again from the back of the café, this time sporting an earpiece with a cord running down his neck and under his collar. When the blond slaps his cell phone shut and heads for the front door I realize the main event is imminent. I can't help thinking the Austrian-born governor might be better served if his staff member wasn't quite so handsome and didn't embody the Hitler youth aesthetic so perfectly.

It is now impossible to move inside the café. Waitresses stop serving and stand attentively behind the bar as I keep my posterior glued to my barstool. The crowd of customers waits in animated anticipation as the decibel level of conversation moves from the hum of chatter to full-out shouting. Outside, in front of the café, everyone is suddenly on his feet and the Schwarzenegger signs supporters carry start bobbing up and down. Through the glass French doors I see the head of the governor come into view.

Photographers, cameramen, and television reporters push into the heart of the sidewalk crowd to get their shot or sound bite. Microphones thrust into the sky and the governor calmly walks a slow but steady course through the throng, shaking hands as he goes. Passing through the front door, he greets Representative Bonnie Garcia who follows him as he makes his way to the back of the room where I sit.

The governor wears a plain white shirt and green gabardine slacks. His face is unlined in a way that can only be achieved through Botox, but if he has had a face lift there are no visible scars. Anyone who rents the documentary *Pumping Iron*, detailing Schwarzenegger's quest for the Mr. Olympia title, will realize the governor's significantly improved Hollywood face bears little resemblance to the distinctly Neanderthal visage on display in that 1977 film. How it got this way is no doubt a fascinating story – and one that will never be told.

The governor has one of the best dye jobs I've ever seen. A warm brown base color is lifted by subtle blond highlights on the top of his head. His hairstyle is a modified pompadour pushed straight back off the forehead, almost concealing the growing bald spot at the back of his head. His skin is perfectly tanned and his white teeth are on prominent display. Handsome and charismatic, the broad-shouldered movie star-turned politico approaches me. He sticks out his massive paw and grabs my hand.

"Thank you for coming out," he remarks, staring me straight in the eye.

Dumbstruck by the unintended double entendre, I shake his hand vigorously and manage to blurt out a response, "Thank you for showing up."

Standing face-to-face with the icon he seems to be just slightly taller than my standard American male height of 5'9", but I will soon discover this is a carefully calculated illusion. The governor continues to move around the room, making his way to the back corner where he stands on a chair to address the crowd. Flashbulbs pop, cameras roll, and the candidate launches into standard campaign rhetoric made palatable by his genuine charm and undeniable charisma. Representative

Bonnie Garcia, also running for re-election in November, beams up a smile as she stands on the floor by his side.

"Thank you all for coming here today," Schwarzenegger shouts. "And thank Representative Bonnie Garcia for all her good work. She is one of our great warriors in Sacramento."

The governor's brief speech continues with a recitation of all he's accomplished since he unseated former Democratic Governor Gray Davis in a recall election two-and-a-half years earlier.

"Col-ee-for-nee-uh is now number one in biotech; number one in stem cell research; number one in job creation; and it has the number one university system in the nation."

As the governor speaks my attention drops to the overdeveloped pectoral muscles moving subtly beneath his crisply ironed white shirt. They have clearly begun to head south, but the governor is smart enough to wear loose fitting clothes that make the effects of gravity less noticeable. The crowd hangs on his every word, cheers go up and a screaming infant is quickly moved out of microphone range. Schwarzenegger finishes his speech with an enthusiastic plea for support in the fall election and begins to retrace his steps toward the front door.

I remain on my barstool facing into the crowd and, in the uncanny way I have of ending up in the middle of things without even trying, the governor walks over and stands next to me, bellying up to the bar and thanking the wait staff for their patience. Still seated with my back to the bar and my knees projecting out from my stool into the room, my thigh is touching that of the governor who is crowded in to my right.

As Schwarzenegger chats with the staff the Honorable Bonnie Garcia lunges forward with a pen in her hand, thrusting her crotch into my knee in the process. The pressure of her groin against my kneecap is relentless and more than a little uncomfortable for me; I cannot look in her face even though it is only inches from my own.

Garcia's arm reaches forward. With pen in hand, she cries out, "Governor, governor."

All the while, Garcia continues to grind her pubis into my kneecap. I know she is unaware of what she is doing and I do not mistake her gesture for a conscious sexual overture. She simply must get Schwarzenegger's attention at any cost. Successful politicians and movie stars can make people to do strange things; when the two are combined in one package temporary insanity is not uncommon.

Garcia leans forward into the governor's side, still riding my knee, and holds out a pen. "Governor, governor," she shouts again.

Schwarzenegger turns his head to the right and takes the pen Garcia offers.

"Please sign a poster for the café owner, he's our host," Garcia asks on her constituent's behalf.

The governor signs the campaign poster for Peabody's owner who stands behind the bar with his waitresses and Garcia backs off. The old adage about politics and strange bedfellows momentarily flashes before my eyes. It will be several months before the Honorable Bonnie Garcia's unconsciousness actions get her into political trouble. Addressing a high school class who asks what she thinks of the governor, Garcia replies, "I wouldn't kick him out of bed." This reply does not go down well with her conservative Republican base.

Schwarzenegger chats with the café owner and waitresses for another moment then turns to face me. Struck with an acute and inexplicable case of Garcia-itis, I thrust my pen into the governor's hand and arch my back like Pamela Anderson at a *Baywatch* reunion, presenting my chest for the governor's consideration.

"For all those bench presses," I suggest, pointing toward my white cotton, v-necked t-shirt.

Without missing a beat The Terminator, the Governor of the State of California, the man who goes down on Maria Shriver, picks up my pen and stretches the cotton tight across my right pectoral muscle. He then proceeds to carefully write his name across my chest. Finishing, he hands the pen back to me with a smile.

At that moment somewhere in the recesses of my mind I manage to call up the images of Cruz Bustamante (California's Democratic Lieutenant Governor and a Schwarzenegger opponent) and Danny DeVito, Schwarzenegger's co-star in the comedy *Twins*. With no premeditation whatsoever I hear the following question fall from my lips.

"If you could replace Cruz Bustamante with Danny DeVito, would you?"

The governor smiles, chuckles, and calmly replies: "Exactly."

I will contemplate this non-answer for several weeks. But while seated at the bar I quickly realize film, politics, sexuality, weight-lifting, journalism, and Palm Springs have all just come together for me in one bright, shining, utterly absurd moment.

The governor swivels and steps forward intending to head for the door, but as soon as he gets even with my knees he is stalled by reporters thrusting microphones in his face and shouting questions. The governor's back is right in front of me and, being the man I am, I let my gaze drop to his formerly bravura rear end and realize it has flattened, like that of most men his age. Then my eyes move downward past the legs of his slacks to his shoes.

The governator wears tan, hand-tooled cowboy boots with a two-inch heel. I have always been good at math. I quickly subtract the height of his boots and pompadour and realize the former bodybuilder and Hollywood action star standing in front of me is 5'7" tall in his stocking feet.

Although we rarely agree on political matters, I respect Schwarzenegger. He gave up an incredibly lucrative career at the age of 55 to start over in an entirely different occupation. Who do I know who would do something like that?

POSTCARD

(1968-1973)

In September, at the age of eighteen, I leave home for Ann Arbor and the University of Michigan. My father agrees to pay for half of my educational expenses if I pay for the rest myself by living at home in the summer and working at the Uniroyal factory in downtown Detroit. He arranges for me to be given two of the worst, heaviest jobs in the factory, first working on the production line as a tire trimmer and then later a tire inspector.

For four long summers I lift everything from steel-belted radials to airplane tires, all steaming hot and delivered directly to my place on the line from the tire presses. The tires pass through the floors of the factory via a series of conveyor belts that are maintained by my father who works as a machinist in the factory. I must wear asbestos gloves to protect my hands from the heat. In my right hand I wield a sharp knife to remove excess rubber from the tire rims. The Uniroyal plant is not air conditioned and summers in Detroit are hot and humid. I stay because that was the deal and because union-negotiated wages for factory workers are twice what I would earn in any of the typical summer jobs available to college students.

I supplement my factory wages with part-time work during the school year as a dishwasher at the University's Mosher-Jordan dormitory. I complete not one, but two majors and graduate with honors. I then finish graduate school without ever needing a student loan.

-10-

Life in the Theater

I've been mulling it over for a few weeks, ever since I saw the little notice in the newspaper. But I blow off the first day of auditions and only decide the evening before the final call that I'm going to show up.

"I need an 8 by 10 head shot," I tell my friend, The Architect, presenting myself at his desk with no advance warning.

"When do you need it?"

"Tonight. Right now. I have an audition tomorrow."

"I see," he drawls laconically.

"Oh come on. All you have to do is point, shoot, and print. It'll just take a few minutes, and I'm not asking you to tart it up in Photoshop. Think of it as one of those Jack Webb just-the-facts-ma'am quickies. I only want them to remember I'm not the cross-eyed hunchback who did a scene from *The Glass Menagerie*. You don't have to make me look like Olivier Martinez."

"Good. I'm not a magician."

Thirty minutes later, armed with my color headshot, I'm sitting at my computer typing out my acting resume. I list my educational credits, my acting experience in Ann Arbor and San Francisco and, in the interests of full disclosure, add the following disclaimer to the bottom of a very short page: "Other than background work this year on location shoots for *Hidden Palms* and *Next*, I haven't had a paying gig as an actor in 20 years." There is simply no point in pretending.

Although I have an undergraduate degree in theater, I stopped acting in 1986. There was no money in it and at the time, my friends were dying by the score. To be a good actor you need to be able to draw on an inner reservoir of feelings and emotion. And in 1986 I was simply too stressed out to do anything beyond go to work in my 9 to 5 job and try to keep myself from going crazy. Emotionally I was shutting down out of self-preservation, and you can't shut down like this and hope to succeed on the stage.

I always thought anyone could be an actor but after seeing several of Madonna's films I realize this is an oversimplification. I love the work but I always hated the life. I had no intention of settling for a string of shitty jobs to support my art while I waited for my big break. And I wasn't going to pretend to be heterosexual offstage for anyone, no matter what sort of glory might await at the end of line. That decision alone would be a career-killer in television or film. Gay or not you can work forever in New York theater, but you're guaranteed to remain slim because the only food you can afford is the stuff you steal from the restaurant kitchen while schlepping plates back and forth from the dining room. So I settled for a different career path, but I always returned to acting.

When I first saw the announcement about the auditions I thought someone had come up with a great idea. The Palm Springs Gay Theater will be a new company, specializing in plays for the gay, lesbian, bisexual, and transgender audience. This seemed terribly smart. As Francois put it in our lunchtime discussion at Look, this town is starved for entertainment. There isn't a single venue presenting gay theater unless you include Tommy Rose's drag revue at Toucan's or the male strippers at Heaven. But Palm Springs has thousands of gay residents, and even more gay visitors who come to stay at the resorts. This seems like an idea whose time has come.

A brief article in one of the gay papers informs me that the theater's founder, Don Jones, is the head of a foundation he established with his late partner. For years they gave out $1,000 stipends to the winners of a literary competition the foundation sponsors for gay playwrights and authors. Now Don is starting a company where some of those works, as well as his own plays, can be produced. He has secured a storefront in a shopping center on the north end of Palm Springs, near the old Racquet Club, and is renovating the former retail space to turn it into a theater.

Don plans an ambitious first season with several productions spread out over six months from November to May. With these auditions he hopes to form a resident company he can draw upon to appear in all the productions. The auditions are being held at the Courtyard Marriott on Tahquitz Canyon, located midway between the airport and downtown.

I arrive late on the second day of auditions, coming straight to the hotel from my workout at World Gym. No stranger to gay theater, I wear my tightest jeans and t-shirt and follow the signs in the lobby to two adjoining conference rooms where the auditions are to take place. In the first room a short, sweet-faced man sits by himself. He asks me fill out a form then escorts me down the hall to the next room. Inside there are three men, all over fifty, sitting behind a banquet table. I shake hands with the man I intuitively sense to be in charge and hand him my head shot and resume. The panel looks like a gay Spanish Inquisition, as envisioned by Mel Brooks.

I am introduced to playwright Victor Bumbalo, the sweet little man who escorted me into the room; Don Jones, company founder and artistic director; Dane Dagger, a curly-haired actor and director; and Dane's lover, Phillip.

"Now if you have something prepared, we'd love to hear it," Don suggests. "Or we have a monologue you can read for us."

With his gray beard and mane of silver hair, Don has a forceful *basso profundo* voice but a gentle disposition. I have a prepared monologue but I decide to ditch it in favor of the cold reading. I like cold readings, because everyone starts as an equal on the same playing field.

"Let me try the reading."

Don hands me a one-page monologue about an older gay man who takes a young boy into his home with the intention of raising him as if he were his son. I focus on the sweetness of the piece, and it seems to work. Don compliments my efforts.

"That was nice. You should have heard some of the stentorian deliveries we got yesterday. Now I'd like to hear you read this."

Don hands me a script for a vaguely S/M seduction scene between two men. Victor reads the other role, seated behind the table while I stand. After we finish Don then asks me to read another two-person scene involving a gay couple who seems to be anticipating the arrival of an adopted child.

As I'm reading the two scenes I have the uncomfortable feeling that I'm about 20 years older than any actor should be to play these parts. In gay theater the opportunities for an actor in his fifties are few and far between. A gay male audience typically wants hot young guys, preferably with their clothes off.

When I finish Don looks at the other inquisitors who nod their heads.

"Can you come back sometime between four and five this afternoon for callbacks?"

"Uh, sure. But could you give me a precise time? I'm pathologically punctual and promise to be here when you want me."

Don laughs out loud, "Well in that case, you're hired. How about five o'clock?"

*   *   *

At callbacks I read with an actor named Mark Burton who has clearly been cast in one of the roles. When I arrive I must wait outside the audition room while another actor reads the same part with Mark that I will read. I've never seen Mark before. A 40-year-old pup, Mark has black hair and brown eyes, a two-day stubble, and a long Welsh face. He is neither exceptionally handsome nor unattractive, and this can be a great asset for an actor because it allows for flexibility in casting.

As soon as we start reading together, I like what happens between us. Mark and I are exactly the same height and weight. Although not quite a gay twin set we make a believable stage couple. More importantly we have good chemistry together. It's hard to define exactly what "chemistry" means when you're talking about actors. But every actor, and every director, knows when it's there; only the delusional think they can manufacture it. I have a little trouble seeing myself in the gay S/M play but the one with the couple adopting the child seems like a good fit.

Mark and I leave the audition together and walk to the parking lot outside the hotel. On the way to our cars, I try to feel him out to see if he's one of the company founders or just another actor.

"So what do you know about this theater company?"

"Not much. I know they plan a whole season starting in November. They seem legit, but they've already asked me if I would consider appearing in the nude."

"Really? What did you say?"

"I said, 'sure.' Actually, it's something I've always wanted to do. Do you live her full time?"

"Yeah, I moved down from San Francisco at the beginning of the year. How about you?"

"I moved here about the same time from Los Angeles."

"Have you done a lot of acting?"

"I tried for a while in L.A., but it really didn't go anywhere. I haven't acted in ten years."

"I'll see you one and raise you one. I haven't acted in twenty."

Mark laughs, "Well, good luck."

As we walk toward our cars, I call back, "I'd wish the same to you, but I can tell from the callbacks you've already been cast."

I like Mark. He seems sweet and genuine. Weeks pass with no word from the new Palm Springs Gay Theater. When I was an undergraduate and didn't get cast in a production I was devastated. Now I know there are many factors behind casting decisions. Talent is only one consideration. An actor must be the right age and type for a role and his physical presence must make a believable contribution to the ensemble. When the phone doesn't ring I don't take it personally. I'm actually kind of proud of the fact that I was both willing and able to walk into an audition, after 20 years away from acting, with no fear whatsoever.

-11-

Universal Divide

I finally get around to closing my San Francisco bank accounts and decide to open a new one at Washington Mutual on the corner of Ramon and South Palm Canyon. I sit in the "new accounts" section of the bank across from skinny Clarence, an unctuous customer service representative. He is obviously a high school graduate, one who takes a banker's responsibilities very seriously.

With his shaved head, high gloss fingernails, and black chinos, Clarence looks like Olive Oyl's younger gay brother. We take an instant dislike to each other. While I'm filling out the necessary paperwork I hear a familiar song on the bank's in-house music system. It's Peggy Lee's original recording of "I Love Being Here with You."

"That's Peggy Lee," I volunteer. "Did you know she wrote that song?"

Clarence looks up briefly then returns to his paperwork without comment.

My first professional assignment as a writer was to meet Peggy Lee then review her performance at the Venetian Room of San Francisco's Fairmont Hotel. She could not have been sweeter to me. We had lunch in Ben Swig's old penthouse at the Fairmont and got along famously. That evening she invited me backstage to her dressing room after the show. Lee ended up liking the article I wrote so much she later sent me a thank you note and asked for permission to make it part of her press kit. Even after her death the piece was still posted on the official Peggy Lee website.

"I love being here with you," I continue. "That's the name of the song Peggy Lee is singing. She wrote it."

Clarence offers a wan smile and I realize twenty years ago he was sucking formula from a bottle while I was lunching with Peggy Lee. It was the end of an era, although I did not realize it at the time. Three years after that luncheon the Venetian Room closed its doors and 45 years of entertainment history came to an abrupt end.

Resuming his duties, Clarence explains, "Now, since you're 55, you qualify for our special senior advantage checking account."

*   *   *

It is insufferably hot. It is hotter than hell; hotter than a Falcon Studios DVD; and hotter than almost any human can stand. I first discovered Palm Springs on a vacation in August of 1978 and fell in love with it immediately, despite the fact that it was 115 degrees when my flight landed. Living all summer in Palm Springs heat, however, is a bit different than enjoying a five-day respite from San Francisco fog.

In the summer, locals stay indoors between noon and 7 p.m. unless they have to commute to work or venture out on some errand that simply cannot be postponed. This month I've noticed myself avoiding looking up at the mountains. In other seasons the mountains surrounding Palm Springs are endlessly fascinating as they turn different colors from morning to night with the changing angle of the sun. But now the intensity of the light is so great I unconsciously look only down or straight ahead to avoid a visual confrontation with the source of the scorching heat. Meteorologists will soon confirm what the locals already know: this July in Palm Springs was the hottest on record, with an average daily high temperature of 107 degrees and a low of 84.6. August is generally hotter.

Heterosexual snowbirds from the North and Midwest avoid summers in Palm Springs like the plague but gay people seem remarkably undeterred by the heat. They continue to vacation in Palm Springs in summer months, taking advantage of the lower off-season rates offered by all the resorts. This month my friend Ed from Los Angeles comes to visit for the week, bringing his chocolate Lab named Arnold. Little Bill and Arnold immediately strike a separate peace, agreeing to co-exist on the living room floor without interacting. Each seems convinced that the other couldn't really be a dog.

I don't feel much like cooking in this heat so Ed and I go out to dinner at our favorite gay hot spots: Wang's of the Desert and El Mirasol. Wang's is a gay Chinese restaurant on Indian Avenue in downtown Palm Springs. The food is good and the restaurant features handsome gay waiters and Latino busboys, with a hopping bar scene for Friday night happy hour. Weekend revelers in shorts and tank tops knock back $2 cocktails, packing Wang's outdoor bar with the kind of big city energy you rarely find in this otherwise sleepy village. All year long Wang's is the gay place to be on Friday nights.

El Mirasol is a Mexican restaurant located on South Palm Canyon on the edge of Deepwell, a predominately gay residential neighborhood. It draws a mixed but mostly gay clientele for reasons I cannot determine other than its central location and a decent menu. Strangely enough, on our nights out at Wang's and El Mirasol, Ed and I are seated at tables near the same man: figure skating coach, Frank Carroll.

In the world of ice skating Frank Carroll is right up there with Dick Button and Peggy Fleming. Now in his late sixties, Carroll has lived in Palm Springs for eighteen years, traveling for coaching assignments and to accompany skaters to competitions. He has coached Michelle Kwan, Sasha Cohen, Evan Lysacek, and dozens of other champions. The curious thing about seeing Carroll in person instead of rinkside on ESPN, is his demeanor.

At both restaurants Carroll's dinner companion is the same much younger man. Their May/December dinners together are essentially silent. Carroll sits stone-faced throughout each meal, never cracking a smile. Yet he does not seem angry. Whatever the pressures of his profession may be, they certainly didn't produce a guy who is a bundle of laughs. Nature or nurture?

*   *   *

On my fifty-sixth birthday I sit with my friend Ed on the terrace at the Sunset Towers Hotel at dusk. Just below us is the swimming pool; beyond that the valley view expands to reveal a panorama of the Los Angeles basin, stretching east to west from downtown to the Pacific Ocean. A carpet of green and white lights sparkles on the valley floor as the orange glow of sunset recedes beyond the horizon line. I love Los Angeles and am always happy here, at least when I'm not required to get in a car and drive somewhere.

Ed is a few years older than I am and he has made different choices. He doesn't work out, he eats and drinks what he wants, and he seems oblivious to his expanding waistline. His job in administration at U.C.L.A. is sedentary and somewhat politically volatile but it works for him. He seems content.

"So tell me," Ed insists, "how does it feel to be fifty-six?"

"I like growing old about as much as Cher likes it. I just hope I'm doing it a little better than she is."

"You Leos are all alike."

"Did you know that I'm a Leo with a Scorpio moon sign and Sagittarius rising?"

"What does that mean?"

I shrug. "How the hell do I know? The guy who did my chart was so confounded by it he couldn't give me a reading. But I remember the puzzled expression on his face when he looked down at his work."

"You mean he didn't tell you anything at all?"

"No. He made one comment. He told me all my signs were in conflict."

"What were you supposed to do with that information?"

"Beats me."

Even in the balmy summer weather of Los Angeles I am cold. I wish I were wearing a jacket over my lightweight sweater. After only a few days' absence I miss the heat of the desert where it is now over 100 degrees each day. I am becoming a desert rat.

*   *   *

I am in Los Angeles to interview Don Spradlin, the promoter behind the second annual Mr. Gay Competition which will take place in Palm Springs this October. Spradlin, a former San Francisco circuit party promoter, is now working out of Los Angeles to gain access to the media outlets he needs to turn his dream project into a marketable international brand.

With his Harvard M.B.A., Spradlin is consulting with a firm that has agreed to provide him with office space and clerical support in their Beverly Hills office to organize the Mr. Gay competition. I stare out a window in the waiting room on the eleventh floor of a Beverly Hills high rise, looking at the Hollywood sign until Spradlin comes out and introduces himself. We shake hands and he leads me to a conference room for our scheduled interview.

I take a seat opposite Spradlin on the other side of his desk. In the hermetically sealed environment of the office tower I feel transported back to 1959. It's a feeling both familiar and unsettling. It doesn't help that Spradlin looks like the actor Carl Betz, who played Donna Reed's husband on *The Donna Reed Show*, and he styles himself accordingly. Clean shaven with closely cropped black hair, Spradlin looks like an older version of the Arrow shirt man or a guy whose face might decorate a box of Grecian Formula for Men. In one way he reminds me of Earl Greenburg. They both exhibit a low key affable demeanor that masks a will of iron and relentless drive.

Originally from Oklahoma City, Spradlin, like Greenburg, did the thing well-educated, upwardly mobile young men of their generation were supposed to do after graduating college. He got married and had children. Fast forward a few decades and the openly gay Spradlin now divides his time between San Francisco and Los Angeles.

Spradlin is in litigation with Donald Trump who recently served him with a cease and desist order for using the brand "Mr. Gay Universe" last year for the inaugural competition. Trump, who owns a controlling interest in the Miss Universe pageant, feels the term "Mr. Gay Universe" violates his trademark. Domestic contestants in what is now known as the "Mr. Gay" contest are now identified first by their city or state name, followed by Mr. Gay (i.e.: San Francisco Mr. Gay, Palm Springs Mr. Gay, Utah Mr. Gay). International contestants, however, can be Mr. Gay Pakistan or Mr. Gay Iran.

Spradlin bristles somewhat when I ask him if the Mr. Gay competition is a beauty pageant.

"No," he replies. "I want to find regular guys. I'm looking for the kind of guy who would never enter a contest like this, someone you might see on the street and not immediately identify as gay. I don't want to present the stereotype of gay men that the world has seen for years."

According to the website for the Mr. Gay competition the mission of the organization is "To raise the visibility of non-stereotypical gay men, humanize gays in the media, and confront homophobia in today's culture."

This is a goal that, on the face of it, would seem hard to debate. But as I press Spradlin on this issue another aspect of his mission becomes clear. Anyone who resembles the late Truman Capote or Matthew Shepard need not apply. But this is not a beauty contest.

Spradlin quickly grasps my objection that the contest could be seen as enforcing a masculine stereotype that is repressive, assimilationist, and intolerant of diversity.

"That's not what I have in mind. I want to reach all those guys like me who are in the closet because they don't see a gay role model they can relate to. I got married and had children and stayed in the closet for years. I want guys who are in the closet to see a positive image of a gay man that makes it seem okay for them to come out. I think the majority of gay men in the world are in the closet."

Spradlin's statement takes me by surprise.

"Are you serious?"

"Yes."

"You really think the majority of gay men are in the closet?"

"Yes."

"That's something I never really thought about."

Since I've been out of the closet my entire adult life it never occurred to me that there was a larger universe of adult males who were gay but closeted. If a guy is presenting himself to the world as straight I usually accept it as his personal truth. But I also remember the old joke: "What's the difference between a straight guy and a gay guy? A six-pack of Bud."

Upon reflection I decide Spradlin may be right, and I don't have to look far into my own coming out process to find support for his point of view. I share my recollection with Spradlin.

"I remember when I realized I was gay in college. I looked at the choices available to me and found it a little depressing. The only images I knew of homosexuals were the stereotypical hairdressers and window dressers. I didn't know what my options would be as a gay man but I knew I didn't want to be a hairdresser or window dresser. That didn't interest me. It was actually kind of scary. There just weren't any gay role models in those days."

"That's exactly the problem I'm trying to address," Spradlin adds. "One of our corporate mottos is 'Gay is not a stereotype.'"

The Mr. Gay competition is a big, expensive, ambitious project that has yet to turn a profit. This year 20 domestic contestants and 20 international contestants are expected to converge on Palm Springs for the October finals. The contestants' online pictures and profiles constitute an alluring assemblage of male pulchritude but I can't help feeling somewhat uncomfortable with the macho tone of what Spradlin proposes. Is it really progressive to resurrect the masculine image of the Eisenhower era? And if that's what we're doing, can we do it without Mamie this time?

Spradlin's cell phone rings and he glances at the identity of the incoming caller.

"Do you mind if I take this?"

"No. Not at all. I need to go to the bathroom anyway."

I return from the restroom just as Spradlin is hanging up.

"Sorry, but that's my date for tonight. He just needed to confirm our plans."

I'm not a betting man, but if I were I'd wager my last dime that the guy on the other end of that phone call is under the age of thirty. But it's none of my business. I decide to change the subject.

"You know, I'm totally into the Miss Universe pageant. I never miss it."

This time it is Spradlin's turn to be surprised.

"Really? What is it you like about it?"

"I think a lot of gay guys are into it. Think about it. Little girls all over the world, from South America, to South Africa, to South Texas, some of them poor and isolated, can watch that show and imagine one day having a crown placed on their head that says they're the most beautiful girl in the world. I think it says something about the universe of the possible and our own ability to reinvent ourselves in a new way. What gay man can't relate to that?"

"Hmmm." Spradlin seems to give the idea serious consideration. "I never really thought about that," he confesses.

*   *   *

According to the official website for Donald Trump's Miss Universe Pageant, "These women are savvy, goal-oriented, and aware. The delegates who become part of the Miss Universe Organization display these characteristics in their everyday lives, both as individuals who participate in the competitions to advance their careers, personal and humanitarian goals, and as women who seek to improve the lives of others." Fortunately for television viewers, Miss Universe contestants are not required to perform a talent competition, unlike the dreadful Miss America Pageant which has become a de facto arm of the religious right and fallen on hard times.

The stakes are higher for Miss Universe. There is a bigger payoff for the winners and competition is stiff. Miss

Universe contestants possess an overtly sexual allure that makes them infinitely more interesting than the goody-two-shoes, God-is-my-co-pilot Miss America Stepford wives. You just know there isn't a single woman on the Miss Universe stage who wouldn't be opposed to offering up a couple of discreet blow-jobs if she thought it would win her the crown. I admire that kind of chutzpah in a woman, especially when she has style. And these women have style.

It's a miserably hot evening in Palm Springs when my friend The Architect and I settle down on the sofa for an evening of babe watching and dish. As always, the contest opens with the parade of nations; each contestant is introduced in a quick close-up wearing a costume inspired by her country of origin.

This year Miss Japan takes the official costume honors. She carries a sword and sports opera length black gloves with a matching black sash tied around the waist of a jungle red mini-dress. The bodice of her national costume is composed of shiny red plastic armor and she sports matching plastic shin guards on her legs. The skirt ends just below her crotch to reveal red window-pane stockings held up by black garters. The overall look suggests a Samurai pole dancer, and we howl with laughter when she is singled-out for the Best National Costume honor.

By the time the 20 finalists are announced we've already picked the winner and it is Miss Puerto Rico. An 18-year-old aspiring actress, Puerto Rico is a knockout who glides across the stage like a cat, rendering the efforts of every other contestant futile when she walks out for the evening gown competition. With long black tresses swept away from a spectacularly beautiful face, Puerto Rico sports a slinky dress made entirely of silver chains, hugging her spectacular body like a second skin. We figure the first runner-up will be Miss Switzerland. At the end of the evening Switzerland turns out to be second runner-up, with Japan taking the first runner-up position. Never underestimate the appeal of a Samurai pole dancer.

But the most remarkable part of the telecast is the appearance of Carson Kressley from *Queer Eye for the Straight Guy*. Given the demographics of pageant-watchers, it's no accident a gay man has been hired to provide color commentary for the telecast. Every gay guy I know loved the first season of *Queer Eye* because it was fresh, original, and gay-positive. And beginning with the second season, everyone I know found the show unwatchable. The reasons behind this gay about-face may be found in the appalling performance of Kressley on the Miss Universe telecast.

Sharing a perch with a former Miss USA, Kressley sits high above the floor of the auditorium, sporting a white tuxedo and holding a microphone. The pageant emcees cut back and forth between the color commentators and the contest for the duration of the evening. Kressley is pancaked, coiffed, and rouged in such a way that he bears a startling resemblance to the late Wayland Flowers' hand-puppet, Madame. Only Madame was twice as butch.

Kressley's commentary is badly scripted and he delivers his lines with the high-pitched, feverish rush of a woman running from a burning building. Things get really terrifying when Kressley goes off book. His ad libs during the show are cloyingly artificial and over the top and he seems like he's on speed. Kressley has clearly succumbed to a terminal case of Paul Lynde Syndrome. Bug-eyed and bombastic, Kressley ramps-up his uber fag persona to stratospheric levels for the pageant and the result is repulsive.

I do not find limp-wristed, nelly, screaming queens offensive – especially when they are clever. As an established cultural stereotype, this persona can still be a refuge for gay men who simply cannot fit comfortably into any other mold. It is the repellant way Kressley panders to the stereotype that makes his Miss Universe participation so disgusting. Whorish and degrading are other adjectives that also come to mind.

Kressley's performance suggests that, on some level, he believes he cannot gain acceptance from the straight world by simply being homosexual; he must BE GAY in a flamboyant way last au courant in the early days of Liberace. This modus operandi is seriously retrograde.

In the era of Denzel Washington, Jamie Foxx, and Morgan Freeman it is neither necessary nor appropriate for a black man to resort to the antics of a Stepin Fetchit in order to secure work in show business. And anyone seriously attempting to embody such an antediluvian stereotype today would be run out of Hollywood on a rail by both blacks and whites. The same standard does not hold today for gay men.

Each time Kressley comes on the screen, The Architect and I roll our eyes in disbelief and sit slack-jawed at his antics. Don Spradlin's butched-up Mr. Gay contest is beginning to seem more prescient with each passing moment.

POSTCARD
(1977)

I am twenty-six. My parents are retired and living once again in Carthage, Tennessee in a home they built after my father was diagnosed with cancer. I have been living in San Francisco with my male lover for over two years when the expected call comes from my mother, announcing my father's imminent death.

An uneventful flight and one-hour drive from the Nashville airport brings me to my parents' house on the banks of the Cumberland River. Returning to Carthage was my father's idea. It has not gone down well with my mother. After forty years of city life she finds the petty provincialism of Carthage stifling, but she was unable to refuse the request of a dying man. A bedside vigil in a town she despises is her reward.

My father is in a coma. What is left of him lies in the hospital connected to oxygen tubes and IVs. My mother and I visit daily, but sometimes only for short periods. Doctors say a patient in a coma, although unable to speak or see, can often hear what is said in his presence. My mother and I are cautioned by the hospital staff to keep this in mind whenever we are in his room. All that is left now is the waiting.

On my final visit to the hospital, I volunteer to sit alone at my father's bedside while my mother goes outside for coffee and a cigarette. His gray skin seems stretched over his skull. The mouth is open, the eyes are closed, and his breathing is labored. From time to time my father tries to clear his voice as if to speak, but I know it is an involuntary reaction to sinus drainage. A device resembling a turkey baster rests on the nightstand for manually suctioning the mucus from the back of his throat.

"It's Robert," I remind him as I reach for the suction device to relieve his distress. I suction a small amount of mucus from his throat and deposit it into a pink, kidney-shaped plastic tray. My efforts do not provide the expected relief.

"It's okay, dad. Just relax."

I stoke his arm with my hand but he continues to struggle with his breathing, for no clear reason.

"Dad, relax. I'm here. It's okay, you don't have to do anything."

Still struggling, his breathing seems to transition into a state of suspended animation. I sense his distress and acting solely on intuition, believe I know what needs to be said.

"Relax. Your work is done. You were a good father."

As soon as the words fall from my lips a sense of peace descends on the room. The labored breathing gives way to a shallow, regular rhythm and my father once again rests calmly. That evening, back at the house, the hospital calls to inform us that my father has died.

My red-eyed mother, exhausted and grief-stricken, lights a cigarette and stares silently into space. After asking me to make the obligatory phone calls to immediate family members she retires to her bed. My final call is to my lover in San Francisco.

As soon as I hear his "hello," I begin.

"Hi. It's me."

I get no further because my voice fails and I begin to cry. I do not cry for the loss of my father. I cry because of the love and tenderness that flows effortlessly in my direction from the man on the other end of the line.

-12-

Life and Stages

I t is Saturday afternoon and the October weather is gloriously sunny and warm. I take Little Bill for a walk and notice the new fountain Bacchanal installed in their perimeter wall a few months ago is temporarily covered by a banner that reads "Orange Coast Leather Assembly." Normally the opening in the wall created for the fountain permits a glimpse into the courtyard and swimming pool of the resort. But not today. I don't think too much about this; it's perfectly clear some leather group has booked the resort for the weekend. I miss the soothing sound of the water passing over rocks and dropping into the basin. As Bill and I pass I realize the fountain is not only covered by the banner but turned off completely.

As Bill sniffs the rose bushes and palm trees outside the wall I hear a strangely familiar, rhythmic sound. It only takes me a few seconds to identify it as the sound of a leather whip being used against flesh. I saw *Gladiator*, okay?

My curiosity gets the best of me and I position myself so I can peer through a crack in the wall to observe the activity. Sure enough, a paunchy, middle-aged man in a leather vest is gently using a leather whip to flog the back of a slave tied to the perimeter wall. The slave remains completely silent; the only sound is the slapping of leather against flesh. Palm Springs is where people come to be themselves or live out a fantasy of who they might be, at least for a weekend.

*   *   *

I receive an e-mail from director Dane Dagger informing me I have been cast as the lead in the one-act play *After Eleven* to be performed this December at the new gay theater company in Palm Springs. I was hoping for a smaller role, considering my 20-year hiatus from acting, but it's only a one-act. As I suspected, Mark Burton will play my lover. I can see myself adopting a baby with him. This should be fun.

I reply with an enthusiastic acceptance and move on to the next e-mail from company director Don Jones. In it he states, "There are also roles in both of the last two shows next spring that I think you could do. But both roles include brief nudity on dimly lit stages. Would you be okay with that?"

Whoa. I'm old enough to appear in the *Palm Springs Follies,* a geezer musical review that's run for ages at the Plaza Theater downtown, and now I'm being asked to perform nude? I don't know what to do with this request. Should I be glad I'm living in Palm Springs, where people actually believe the prospect of seeing a 56-year-old man naked will cause people to buy tickets instead of ask for a refund? I decide the only smart answer for the moment is "maybe."

As soon as I hit the SEND button replying to Don's e-mail my phone rings. It's Dane Dagger.

"Welcome aboard."

"Thanks. I'm really excited about acting again."

"That's great. We'll be the second show of the season, opening on December 28. But I'm calling because I have an idea I want to propose. We're going to do Victor's one-acts, *Kitchen Duty* and *After Eleven* back-to-back separated by an intermission. We think it would be really good for you and Mark to play the lead roles in both plays. You would be one character in the first play and a different one in the second. It could be the chance for some real tour de force acting."

I immediately realize it is a good idea and a great opportunity for an actor. My ego leaps into the void.

"Wow! That sounds like fun. I think I can handle it."

"Great the first read through is at my house in two weeks. It'll be fun. In the first play you'll play the leather man. How do you look in chaps?"

The leather man? THE LEATHER MAN? What have I gotten myself into?

* * *

The press luncheon for the Mr. Gay competition is held at Azul, a restaurant on North Palm Canyon. It is set up as a buffet with lots of time for journalists to meet and greet contestants. When I arrive Don Spradlin smiles at me from across the room and waves, but the vibes suggest he's really giving me the stink eye. My story on the competition inferred, with little subtlety, that the whole endeavor might be the gay male equivalent of an Aryan race movement.

Outside on the patio forty contestants fresh from a rock climbing competition knock back cocktails and get to know each other. I run into Mayor Ron Oden and we chat for a while. I like Oden. He has an affable, easy going demeanor and seems to genuinely care about Palm Springs. At City Council meetings he speaks his mind and votes his conscience. The worst thing I can say about him is that he sometimes gets a little verbose, but this should be expected from a man who was a Seventh-day Adventist minister in the years when he was closeted and married to a woman.

"Look at these guys," I suggest to Oden. "They're all so young and cute. I feel like Father Time around here today."

Oden, who is my age and nicely put together, shoots me a reality check.

"Yeah, but I remember the men who were so cute and popular when I was in my twenties. Not many of them still looked that way 20 years later."

"You're right. That's exactly what I needed to hear. I guess we're not doing so badly after all."

I take a seat at a cocktail table, park my Diet Coke, and the publicist begins to shuttle men over to my table for a chat. My first request is for my two favorites from the competition website: Mr. Italy, Fabio Falco, who comes accompanied by his translator, Mr. Vatican City, Francesco Mondavi. Fabio speaks no English, but Francesco, an architect, has lived in Los Angeles for years.

They are Frick and Frack, with Mr. Vatican City a super skinny 6'4" and Mr. Italy a hunky 5'7".

They smile constantly and are clearly having the time of their lives. Francesco met Don Spradlin at a West Hollywood party and Spradlin recruited him for the competition. Francesco originally entered under his own name, adopting Francesco only when he found out he was going to be interviewed for Italian *Vanity Fair*, which his mother always reads. He hates the Catholic Church and actually wrote them directly, requesting they mail him the paperwork for ex-communication.

Fabio, who is from Rome, answers my questions through Francesco, who is wonderfully paternal toward his short doppelganger. Together they look like the gay Italian version of a young Fred Astaire and Gene Kelly.

Fabio explains, "I entered the competition because I thought it would be a different experience and a good reason to leave Italy and explore a new place. I want to work as an actor."

"Don't you think being Mr. Gay might hurt your chances in Italy?"

"I don't think so."

"Does your mother know you're Mr. Gay Italy?

"Yes, my parents found out I was gay by accident when I won the Mr. Italy competition. They never watch television and don't have cable but I gave an interview to a cable station in Rome. That week, my parents took advantage of a promotion for a free week of cablevision. While they were channel-flipping they ran across my interview. So that was it."

The revolving door of contestants led to my table includes Mr. Gay Australia, a dancer, who parades around in an exotic pirate-inspired costume provided by his fashion designer sponsors. Mr. Lichtenstein is actually a German who was working in Lichtenstein on a journalism internship when the competition came up. His two sisters both competed in the Miss Germany pageant for the Miss Universe contest.

"It's not about winning," he explains. "It's about being here. It's a big family. I like all the guys." He just got here yesterday and he's sponsored by Generation X – an agency that produces music events and the Northern Germany Mr. Leather contest.

Mr. Iran lives in Canada but was born in Iran and has dual citizenship. After we finish our interview he comes back and asks me not to use his surname in print. Mr. Morocco speaks English, French, and Arabic and lives in Holland right now where he is majoring in child psychology and Islamic studies. He is Muslim but his parents don't know he is gay. He lives with his mother and she doesn't read papers or watch TV. He'd like to work for gay people in Morocco, where right now you can't come out as gay.

Hunky Mr. Israel, attorney Nathan Shaked, is in his mid thirties and older than most contestants. He owns eight fitness clubs in Israel where he lives. Friendly, butch, and sexy, Shaked is rather full of himself.

It is impossible to talk to forty guys in the allotted time and I find myself drawn exclusively to the international contestants. Because I know American guys so well, they don't interest me as much. But Mr. Anchorage proves himself the exception. He's a bit overweight and no beauty, but a really nice guy. He also finds himself housed in a resort for gay bears that is clothing optional.

"I guess it was the beard that made them put me there," he speculates. "But I haven't been hanging around nude. There are only two other guys there right now. When I signed up for the competition I didn't really imagine myself hanging around with a couple of naked bears around a swimming pool."

*   *   *

For the first time since the Palm Springs Film Festival, I'm back at the Palm Springs Convention Center for the Mr. Gay USA Competition which is not being held in the large main hall. Mr. Gay will be crowned in the Primrose Room, a banquet room at the north end of the Convention Center. The room is large and configured with V.I.P. tables up front near the stage. The V.I.P. section has tablecloths and an open bar. The rest of the room has neat rows of chairs and is separated from the V.I.P section by low curtains suspended from aluminum divider pipes about three-feet high. The emcee for both nights of the competition is Bruce Vilanch and the judges include gay gossip columnist Billy Masters, actor/director Dirk Shafer, and Dennis Hensley, author and one of Kathy Griffin's recently fired official "gays."

Outside in the lobby Don Spradlin paces back and forth like an expectant father holding a vigil outside the delivery room. I stop and ask him for an update on some contestants who never arrived.

"Well, Mr. Venezuela turned out to be an imposter who sent in someone else's photo for the competition. He refused to provide his own passport photo to verify his identity. Mr. Iraq didn't work out because of the immigration difficulty. The logistics of bringing him in through Canada became too difficult and I was afraid he would request political asylum as soon as he arrived at the border and never show up for the competition."

Inside the hall attendance is sparse for the Mr. Gay USA event. Only about 30% of the seats are filled. There are about 300 people in attendance, including the judges and production staff, with three videographers and two still photographers.

I have time to run backstage where the contestants are segregated into domestic and international competitors. The USA contestants compete tonight; the international competitors are only here this evening to fill the stage and give the audience a glimpse of the entire collection. I have unofficially adopted Francesco and Fabio, Mr. Italy and Mr. Vatican City, because they are adorable and fun.

Hanging with the international contestants, I ask the group, "So, you guys have been here for 48 hours. Did anyone get laid yet?"

A resounding reply of "No!" arises from the crowd, with lots of laughter and some amazement at their own failure to perform up to the gay male expectation. No one seems to be faking their denial.

Fabio adds, "My family can't believe I haven't scored since they say I'm such a whore."

I move on to Mr. Germany who is half Egyptian, half German, and all beautiful. He lives in Frankfurt and speaks perfect English. I take a photo as the guys are given their two-minute warning.

Back in my front row seat, I watch as the international contestants come out first, followed by the Americans. Bruce Vilanch is dressed like a fugitive extra from *Brokeback Mountain* in a white western shirt, jeans, boots and cowboy hat. The contestants all wear jeans and casual shirts. Vilanch is funny and incredibly quick. The American contestants are handed out roses by the current Mr. International Gay and asked to give a rose to the man they feel should be Mr. Congeniality. Mr. Anchorage, who impressed me earlier as a sweetheart, takes the honors.

The ten domestic finalists are chosen then asked to pull a question from a basket that Vilanch will read. Mr. Boston, the crowd favorite and clearly the most beautiful man on stage, completely blows the simple question, "Who is your hero?" He goes blank for such a long time Vilanch has to start vamping in an attempt to cover. Boston is so uncomfortable and awkward it is embarrassing. And he is a man who is not only physically stunning but who graduated from Harvard last year.

The next step in the competition is a bizarre aerobics demonstration in which the ten finalists come out in bicycle shorts and tank tops to perform one minute of jumping jacks, sit ups, and tumbles. Mr. Sacramento stands out by executing a series of back flips, but most of the contestants seem embarrassed by this part of the competition.

An intermission follows in which everyone but me and a few others file out to the lobby to purchase drinks. One of the production staff members comes along and begins removing the low black curtains that hang from the barriers that separate the main seating section from the V.I.P. tables.

I tell him, "But if you take those down, the contestants will be able to see us masturbating."

He instantly takes one of the black curtains he has just removed and arranges it around my waist to cover my lap. Everyone within earshot breaks out laughing.

In the second half, the finalists come out in swimsuits and Vilanch announces the next phase of the competition where the contestants raise money for The Trevor Project, a non-profit foundation that assists gay and questioning youth and helps prevent teen suicide. The disco music begins and the contestants jump from the stage and go out into the audience to dance for dollars, which even judges begin stuffing into their trunks. Suddenly the competition has turned into a bump and grind show. The only things missing are brass poles and Plexiglas high heels.

Mr. Sacramento finally wins the title of Mr. Gay USA. Walking slowly toward my car, beneath the beautiful swooping colonnade of the convention center, I'm still trying to distill the essence of what I've just witnessed. The thing that most stands out is the sweetness of the whole thing, the corny gay male silliness that overshadows the big biceps and tiny swimsuits.

*   *   *

The following afternoon I arrive early to watch the international contestants rehearse. The guys are all in casual clothes going through the motions for tonight's event with the choreographer and director, a man who has programmed female beauty pageants for years.

Fabio is being a totally goofball clown, wearing a pair of workout shorts and pulling at his penis in the unself-conscious, time-tested Italian tradition. He cannot be corralled into submission by the director who must constantly call out his name and insist he stop talking. But the chatter continues even though Fabio basically speaks no English. Francesco, Mr. Vatican City, is being an absolute angel, assuming the volunteer role of Fabio's translator, mentor, and foster parent.

Fabio constantly calls out to Francesco for help, like a five-year-old asking his father to come see his latest creation or solve his newest puzzle. Right now he needs a shirt and pants for the tonight's competition tonight because he doesn't have anything he feels is nice enough.

Fabio and Francesco are friendly and cordial and I volunteer to bring Fabio a shirt or two for tonight. He can try them out and see if he likes them. I also remind him, "And Fabio. In America, no…" I tug aggressively at my penis. "In Roma, si, but in America no." I pull at my penis again and Fabio beams his big Italian smile and strips down to his underwear to put on a pair of borrowed pants. Then he calls out to Francesco in Italian, asking for a belt. Francesco translates the request and calls out to the guys in a loud voice, "Fabio needs a belt."

Mr. Australia comes through with a black leather one he hands to Francesco for delivery.

One of the producers of the show is standing around with a friend, also watching the antics. With a laugh, he turns to me and remarks, "The gay factor certainly comes alive in person, doesn't it? Much more than you would expect just from looking at the photos on the website."

He's right. When the guys get together in a group, despite Don Spradlin's desire that Mr. Gay should be the kind of guy no one would pick as gay, there could be no doubt in the mind of any observer just what the common denominator might be.

*   *   *

In early evening I show up backstage at the convention center with two shirts for Fabio. He is like a puppy, with all the out-of-control energy and unrestrained enthusiasm of a Jack Russell terrier. He declines an elegant French silk shirt that I brought but elects to wear a short-sleeved black and white stripe Calvin Klein. He tries it on and looks 100% better in it than I ever will. I take a picture with him and Francesco.

Outside in the lobby before the international competition begins, I once again run into Ron Oden. He taps me on the shoulder in the lobby and asks, "So what do you think of the event?"

"I've been spending a lot of time with the guys since yesterday morning and I'm so impressed with how sweet they are, how non-competitive. Everyone seems to be having such a good time and they're so nice to each other. They're pretty easy on the eyes, too."

"That's good to hear," Oden adds. "It wasn't that way last year."

Oden was a judge at last year's inaugural competition and he continues to explain.

"There was one guy who thought he should have won and when he didn't, he got so pissed-off he refused to pose for photographs with the other contestants."

Oden is quickly steered away by a couple of audience members who insist on a photo with the mayor. He obliges and I return to the auditorium.

The contest ends with 37-year-old Nathan Shaked, the Israeli attorney/fitness club owner taking the Mr. Gay International title. His aggressive, hyper-masculine demeanor makes him a curious choice from my point of view. From the moment I first saw him he brought only one thing to mind: a Colt model. I don't know if Spradlin is looking for this type as an antidote to the nelly queens he seems so repelled by, but it is what the judges for the international competition give him. But I still wonder if substituting one gay stereotype for another constitutes progress.

When I go backstage after the competition to collect my shirts, Fabio's daffy smile is gone and his big brown eyes are downcast. He neither won nor placed in the top five, although Francesco was second runner-up in the finals. Fabio sheepishly removes my shirt and places it on a hanger. In English, he says "thank you." I give him a hug and grab Francesco so the three of us can have our picture taken together. But I pass on the after party at Heaven. I decide the contestants will enjoy it more if their self-appointed gay uncle is not hanging around in the background.

The evening is warm and beautiful as I walk home with two shirts thrown over my shoulder. A half-moon illuminates the mountain crest and the smell of smoke is no longer in the air. For the last two days the largest California wildfire in five years has consumed thousands of acres on the other side of the mountains. Five firefighters die when they are trapped in their truck by the flames. Set by an arsonist, this unnatural disaster is known as the Esperanza fire. Esperanza is a small town in the mountains and the Spanish word for hope.

-13-

Another Opening, Another Show

Aﬁer breakfast I pull out the script for the upcoming production of *Kitchen Duty* and *After Eleven* on the doormat. I grab a highlighter and begin reading, marking my dialogue as I go. The opening play, *Kitchen Duty*, is set in the1970s. It begins as a seduction scene in which a hunky leatherman picks up a younger guy on Christopher Street and brings him up to his apartment for a bondage scene. After he restrains the guy with handcuffs and leg cuffs, he realizes he doesn't have the key to remove them. This provokes an asthma attack in the younger man whose ex-lover must be called to bring his medication. Although dated, the play is well written and can work if it's performed as a period piece. The dialogue is funny and the stage directions include lots of complicated stage business involving the leg and handcuffs.

Having read only three pages at the auditions, I thought the second play, *After Eleven*, was about a couple anticipating the arrival of their adopted child. Instead I discover it is about a couple in an eleven-year relationship, awaiting the arrival of the hustler they've hired to spice up their relationship. The man who arrives is a novice and the anticipated ménage never materializes. But the encounter provokes a funny and timeless exploration of the dynamics between long-term partners.

I'm impressed with the quality of Victor Bumbalo's writing, and I'm comfortable wearing chaps and appearing shirtless in the first play. As best I can recall, I'm a good actor. I remember the old adage, "dying is easy, comedy is hard," but I know how to play comedy. And I think I can create two distinctly different characters and perform them back to back in the same evening.

My panic attack only begins when I fan through the 80 pages of the script and look at the amount of highlighter. One-third of all the dialogue is mine. In addition I have a two-page soliloquy in *After Eleven* I must deliver into a telephone. Oh my God. I haven't memorized that much dialogue in 20 years. Do those circuits still exist in my brain? This speculation leads directly to the bottom of my personal well of insecurity and the thought that my performance might turn out like an *American Idol* audition, the sort of hideous embarrassment looped endlessly on shows like

Entertainment Tonight and *Access Hollywood* as the nonpareil of incompetence.

The cast convenes for the first read-through at the director's house in Cathedral City. Dane lives with three cats, his lover of over 20 years, and a third partner who seems to be a recent addition to their sexual landscape. It's more information that I want, but I figure Dane should at least understand the comedic landscape of the second play.

Dane has a rotund face and body, brown Orphan Annie curls, and a positive energy that is reassuring. He's been acting and directing in community theaters for decades. The ex-lover in *Kitchen Duty* will be played by Matt, a local actor/singer/masseur with a barrel chest and big voice. The hustler of *After Eleven* will be played by Brandon, a sweet, smart family therapist with an incredible bubble butt and big biceps. Brandon is the least experienced actor in the company, and it shows, but he is also the nicest guy.

Cats stalk and circle the table where we read and once we're finished, Dane hands us the rehearsal schedule which is five weeks long. We will meet three or four days each week and rehearse in three-hour sessions. Five weeks, 80 pages. Oh, God.

The read-through goes well and physically we're all the right "types" for the roles in which we have been cast. We are not all the right ages, however, a fact that is omnipresent in my brain. Each of us is at least a decade older than the characters should be for these plays. I gently point this out to the director.

"Oh that doesn't matter," Dane says reassuringly. "This is the Palm Springs. Everyone is older here. The audience won't even notice."

I'm trying not to freak. I remind myself this is a new company in a small theater on the edge of a California desert. But from bedroom to boardroom, I've never been able to do anything with less than 100% concentration. I approach everything as if it were the pinnacle of my long and illustrious career and the crowning achievement of my life. Weird and somewhat scary, I know, especially for me. We're scheduled as the second show of the theater's debut season but I've driven by the theater space and there doesn't seem to be anything happening at the site.

Somewhat disingenuously I ask Dane, "How are the renovations going on the theater space?"

"Right now I think they're in plan check," he replies.

Plan check? All my bells and whistles go off. Having bought, sold, and remodeled many properties, and worked with Palm Springs contractors, I know exactly where this is headed. Palm Springs contractors are a special breed of non-performers. A good local building contractor is a rare find, and since the Coachella Valley is a boom town for builders; the good ones are usually booked a year in advance. What you have left are the dregs. Their concept of time is so vague it simply cannot be quantified. They don't show up, don't return calls, and don't adhere to a schedule. I immediately know the theater space is never going to be ready for the planned mid-November debut production.

Dane adds, "Don is saying if the theater isn't ready for the planned opening date, he'll cut the first show and move it to the end of the season. If that happens, we'll be the debut show for the company."

"Trust me," I add. "We'll be the debut show."

"I don't know the specifics and I'm going to stay out of it," Dane declares emphatically. "I've run several theater companies as artistic director and I'm finished with all that. Directing is just fine for me at this point in my life. I don't need the headaches of all those additional responsibilities."

*   *   *

Rehearsals begin in earnest at Don Jones' house because the theater is under construction and unavailable. The first play is now officially canceled and we are confirmed as the opening show. Don's house is in a gated "active adult community" for people over the age of 55. When I learn about Don's background I begin to see "active adult community" in a new way, half anticipating it to be adjacent to a "passive adult community."

Don, in addition to being a playwright, produced gay porn when he was living in Manhattan in the 1970s. Using Dane to float the proposal, Don gets both Mark and Matt to agree to some gratuitous frontal nudity for our production. Although now older and in ill health, Don's fundamentally lecherous bent remains. He is also the man spending almost $100,000 to create a new theater and he's smart enough to know sex sells tickets, especially when your target is a gay male audience.

I pick up Mark, my on stage lover, and we drive over to Don's house for the first rehearsal. When we pull up to the guard house in front of the gates, I roll down my window and a uniformed blond woman leans out over the bottom half of a Dutch door.

"We're going to Don Jones' house," I announce, "for a rehearsal."

"Oh yes," she replies, with a pronounced Irish brogue. "You're the *Barber of Seville* boys. I expect to hear your voices floating out over the desert in a few moments. Go right through."

Mark and I smile and nod in her direction as the electric gates part.

Pulling the car forward, I hiss to Mark, "*Barber of Seville?* Why did he tell them we're rehearsing *The Barber of Seville?*"

"God knows," replies Mark, with a roll of the eyes.

Dane and Don are waiting for us inside Don's house. A quick tour of the interior reveals the home as a strange reinvention of a Spanish tile-roofed saloon, with lots of rounded interior arches. The bedroom has a curious wainscoting of paneling, almost making Don's four-poster bed and Victorian settee look appropriate, if only we weren't in the middle of the California desert in the 21st Century. Don's collection of chinoiserie is on display in various nooks and crannies, and his living room looks like the remains of an Arkansas trailer park just after the tornado passed through.

Don's two rescued dogs, Killer and Diller, are mutts of the basic German Shepard/Rottweiler persuasion and totally out of control. Don is now the one who needs rescuing. New when purchased, the home currently features wall-to-wall carpeting littered with dog feces. And since Don is a heavy smoker the entire house reeks of cigarettes. Killer and Diller jump all over us as Mark and I make our way into the living room. The floor is covered with torn paper from the Yellow Pages, recently shredded with a vengeance by Don's in-house canine tag-team.

"Here," he says, handing a broom to Mark and a black Hefty bag to me. "I can't bend down to pick up all this crap, so if you'll just clean up first we can get started."

Wait. Wait just a minute. Where are the dulcet tones of an assistant director, suggesting that someone invite Mr. Julian onto the set? Mark and I look at each other, stifle our revulsion, and silently begin the clean-up process.

"I just can't seem to keep a housekeeper," Don laments.

The first order of business is to take publicity photos in an approximation of what we'll be wearing in the show. Don is the photographer and Mark strips down to the towel he'll wear to open the second play. Matt and Brandon arrive and Brandon puts on a robe. Matt sports a sweatshirt and I put on the wife beater I'll remove at the end of the first play. Beefcake or cheese? I struggle to repress this kind of speculation but I can't seem to stem the tide. As we position ourselves in various states of soft core dishabille for Don's digital camera, I hope for the best.

Four of our five weeks of rehearsal will take place in what we all come to refer to as Stench House, and the working conditions never improve. Each night I have to stop and open the sliding glass door of the living room several times for a dose of breathable air. And we always arrive to face a clean-up task that includes picking up doggie doo-doo and the stuffing and fabric Killer and Diller have torn from Don's sofa and chairs. By the end of the month he will have to replace all his living room furniture.

Our resentment at executing housekeeping tasks before rehearsal is worn down by the experience of stepping in dog feces on nights when we haven't done a thorough reconnaissance of the living room floor. Mark, who is barefoot in the first play, is the first to grasp the necessity of continued intervention. Whenever we forget, there is always an unpleasant reminder.

Early in the rehearsal process Mark suggests we get together and run lines outside of scheduled rehearsals or we'll never master all of our dialogue. The two actors in supporting parts have smaller, easier jobs playing only one character each. The responsibility for pulling off these plays in performance rests squarely on our shoulders.

*   *   *

Mark accurately describes the entry gates of his Palm Springs gated community as looking like the entrance to Jurassic Park. The development is something of a non-sequitur for Palm Springs. It contains luxury single-family residences on large lots, surrounded by a tall stucco perimeter wall. And although the homes, built in 1999, have no particular architectural distinction, they all sell for over $1 million.

This sort of community is more common in the east valley Republican enclaves of Palm Desert and La Quinta. It's the sort of place where people willfully cut themselves off from the outside world and, hopefully, its problems. These carefully controlled environments offer abundant square-footage, tall ceilings, Sub-Zero refrigerators, and kitchens and bathrooms with marble and granite. But they reflect only a rudimentary understanding of architecture and design; their buyers mistakenly accept the assumption that costly materials and high-end appliances infer distinction. In the parlance of architecture, they do not even rise to the level of "decorative."

The vaguely Mediterranean façade of Mark's home with its covered portico, recalls the upper middle-class suburban prisons of Douglas Sirk movies. Every time I pull into Mark's cul de sac I expect to see Dorothy Malone peering out from behind a ruffled curtain, clutching a dirty martini and scrutinizing the arrival of an unexpected visitor.

Mark is a house-husband who lives with Jack, his partner of seven years. Jack is a regional manager with a large national real estate company. He is nice, boring, he walks like a duck, and he has arrived at his mid forties without ever having traveled outside the United States. Jack has worked in real estate all his adult life and his mid six-figure salary eliminates the need for employment on Mark's part. This is not an arrangement that arose by accident but a clearly defined negotiated agreement.

With Jack at the office, Mark and I meet at his house regularly during the week to run lines and get comfortable with Dale's blocking of the plays. On one of our earlier meetings Mark volunteers a little background on his relationship.

"I was working for this mom and pop accounting firm in the San Fernando Valley when Jack and I started dating. For seven years I was their only employee and I hated the work. They had a lot of celebrity clients, including Faye Dunaway."

"Everyone I know who had any professional dealings with her says she's the consummate bitch."

"They're right. I once got so angry with her I screamed at her over the phone and slammed the receiver down in her ear. It takes a lot to get me to that point."

"So Jack agreed to take you away from all that."

"Basically. I told him I always wanted to be like a fifties housewife, that kind of *Ozzie and Harriet, Father Knows Best* home-maker. And Jack was fine with that."

I "get" Mark on some fundamental level and know the truth is more complex. At forty, Mark is nice, positive, and never bitchy or deliberately mean. He is also a grand mal manipulator who tends toward indecisiveness and is the consummate procrastinator. Mark didn't finish college, didn't finish interior design school, didn't stick with his singing lessons, didn't stay with acting, and after taking classes for months stopped cooking altogether. He and Jack now go out for dinner every night. This behavior doesn't quite fit the image of the 1950s housewife Mark initially sold to Jack. But Jack doesn't seem to mind.

Mark's two concessions to domesticity are elaborate Christmas decorations inside and outside the home that he personally executes over a period of weeks each year, and laundry. Mark does copious amounts of laundry, partly as a result of the Lady Macbeth complex he has about bedding. He not only washes all the sheets and pillowcases for their four-bedroom house, but he carefully irons them before putting them on the bed.

Mark and I work regularly on our lines in the family room adjacent to his kitchen. For the complicated stage business in the first play, Mark purchases keyed leg and handcuffs so we can get comfortable using them. Wearing them helps him with his stage movements. I, in turn, must practice seducing him while he is confined. I do not find this task objectionable. My opening line in the first play is, "Take that shirt off." Things evolve from there.

As our blocking comes together and the lines become more comfortable, I find myself doing what the director and the script require: kissing Mark passionately in an attempt to seduce his character into cooperating with my character's bondage fantasy. My character really starts coming together as soon as I get a cold and my voice drops two octaves. Working in that register is perfect for the leather man. His physical stance and movements quickly fall into place as soon as I put on the knee-high leather engineer boots I will wear under the chaps. They are transformational, inducing an automatic swagger and causing me to thrust my pelvis forward when I walk.

Early in our private rehearsals I find myself pulling Mark toward me with force and determination. My own persona slips involuntarily in to the vortex of the leather man and is consumed. Mark responds with an enthusiasm that exceeds the level of cooperation indicated in the stage directions. With simultaneous erections stiffening inside our jeans, pages of dialogue fall from our occupied hands and settle on the floor as a deep, Barry White growl begins in my chest and rolls its way to my throat. In the character voice that will soon become second nature for me I whisper an unscripted promise into Mark's ear.

"I will never make you write bad checks or ask you to leave your husband."

Mark's laundry does not get done that day.

*   *   *

We have our first run through in the theater and we're all surprised by what a little jewel box Don created. He and his contractors built a smart, welcoming 45-seat venue for live performance. The author, Victor Bumbalo, drives in from Los Angeles for this rehearsal and the technical crew works with us for the first time, writing down prop placement and fixing light cues.

Local CBS television Channel 2 comes to shoot a segment for their evening entertainment news magazine, *Eye on the Desert*. Andi, the female roving reporter, travels with a microphone and her own cameraman. We give her the requested sound bites and perform a few moments from the second play. It's all wrapped in less than 15 minutes and results in three minutes of air time.

But the most extraordinary event of the evening is the private moment I have on stage before the camera crew arrives. I walk into the theater as the contractors are applying the last bit of paint, hanging lights, and preparing the backstage area. When I stand in the middle of the stage it hits me. For the first time in 20 years I get that feeling an actor gets in his gut when he stands alone on stage in an empty theater. It doesn't happen consistently but every actor knows the experience. Your stomach feels light and hollow and hair rises on the back of your neck as you grasp, on a completely visceral level, that this is a place where magic happens. It is part of a tradition at least 2,000 years old. For many people, especially actors, the theater is a place holier than any cathedral. The human comedy, in all its variety, unfolds on the stages of the world every night.

A week after our first rehearsal in the theater, a group of 15 volunteers from the Desert AIDS Project and some actors cast in upcoming company productions attend our final dress rehearsal. It is a good show, with everyone hitting their marks and laughter coming in all the right places. There are only a few fluffed lines which we disguise pretty effectively.

*   *   *

It is the afternoon on the day our show opens. Mark, Dane, and I rendezvous downtown for an hour-long talk radio interview with local entertainer Joey English. That evening when I arrive at the theater there are flowers for each cast member on our dressing room tables from Don and Dane, with notes of congratulations and good wishes. I give Mark a sterling silver heart-shaped keychain with a dangling heart charm. I have engraved the names of our characters in *After Eleven* on the heart. Mark gives each cast member a $20 Starbucks gift card.

The theater sparkles and the house manager and staff are dressed in white shirts and bow ties. At intermission they pour champagne for the audience. Although the performances will mature and improve with the length of our run, we know we've pulled it off. Half-way into our month-long schedule, we start selling out every performance, sometimes with audience members occasionally sitting on stage to accommodate overflow crowds. Palm Springs now has a new gay theater company.

Several times in this process I questioned whether this pursuit was worth the extraordinary investment of time. I stayed because I recalled the time in 1980 when I was cast in a play at Theater Rhinoceros, which was at the time a fledgling gay San Francisco theater company located in the Goodman Building on Geary Boulevard. That theater, like the new gay theater company in Palm Springs, was in a storefront. San Francisco's Theater Rhinoceros is now thirty years-old, and the longest running gay theater company in the world.

For one month I am a minor celebrity in Palm Springs. I get recognized at supermarkets and car washes by guys who seem genuinely enthusiastic about our production. I cannot see the audience when I'm on stage but one of my friends comes to the show and later remarks, "Your audience is made up of older gay couples who live here full time but never go out to the gay bars or clubs."

The biggest compliment I receive for our efforts comes from a guy I run into at the gym. He stops me in the middle of my workout to say how much he enjoyed my performance. Then he adds, "It's so nice to have a theater here in Palm Springs that reflects our lives. Until this company opened, we didn't have that."

POSTCARD

(1992)

I am forty-one. My boyfriend and I attend a screening of *A League of Their Own*, a charming and beautifully cast motion picture directed by Penny Marshall. The film is a true story based an all-female baseball league from the 1940s. Sitting in the balcony of San Francisco's Kabuki Theater, I watch the final moments of the film, when the real women from the original baseball team are reunited and introduced to the actresses who portray them in the film. The reunion of the older women takes place on a baseball diamond. For most viewers it is a moment of nostalgia. It wraps-up the lives portrayed in the film, brings the viewer up to date, and reinforces the reality of the story. For me it is something else entirely.

Tears instantly fill my eyes as the first gray-haired ladies enter the frame. As more women gather to greet each other, a groundswell of anger, resentment, hurt, grief, and loss all coalesce somewhere in my gut. The trickle of tears turns into a torrent as I begin to sob uncontrollably – big, shoulder-heaving bursts of emotion I cannot control. This is a crying jag, one of those maudlin displays of sentiment usually reserved for the graveside of a loved one as the casket is lowered into the ground.

I bury my face in my hands as the credits scroll across the screen, finding it impossible to speak or stop crying. My date puts his arm around my shoulder and tentatively inquires, "What is it? What's wrong?"

I cannot respond. The theater empties before I am able to wipe away the tears with my shirt sleeve and croak a reply.

"We'll never have a moment like that, even if we live to be that old. By that time most of our friends will be dead."

When ushers arrive to clean the theater before the next screening I rise from my seat and stumble up the aisle with the assistance of my friend. I suppose this is what some people might describe as a manifestation of "post traumatic stress syndrome." I am still waiting for the "post" part.

-14-

Closing Credits

Y ou were a good father. I knew I was lying when I uttered those words beside my father's deathbed. He was a complete failure as a parent in every way that counts to a child. Yet this did not stop my mother from beginning the posthumous canonization of his memory immediately after his death.

Years later, my mother and I are dining at the home of my Aunt Mary when my mother embarks on one of her fictional reveries about my late father.

"Oh, my, he certainly loved children," she sighs.

Aunt Mary unexpectedly adds, "Except his own."

Silence follows Aunt Mary's proclamation. But when my mother excuses herself to go to the bathroom I thank my aunt for giving me the only validation I have ever received about what I always knew to be true.

My father was an unwanted child. His mother died when he was four years old and my grandfather quickly married a woman who, once she had two children of her own, had no interest in being saddled with her husband's son from a previous marriage. My father was uneceremoniously dumped into the home of the only in-laws willing to take him. He grew up without the love and acceptance of nurturing parents, and therefore he had no role models for this sort of behavior.

In 1953, when I was three, my paternal grandfather killed himself. His body was found dangling from a rope, suspended from a rafter in the warehouse of the family business. After his funeral my father had a nervous breakdown. The psychiatrist who attended to him told my mother, "he's a tough nut to crack," essentially acknowledging his failure. My father only agreed to see the therapist twice and the only advice he took from the man was to take up a hobby. He took up fishing. My dad graduated from the school of hard knocks, summa cum laude, but with permanent scars.

I eventually came to understand my father's journey. And when I sat beside his deathbed, forgiveness, not vengeance was on my mind. So I lied. Maybe that lie brought some peace of mind to his final hours. I certainly hope so. The gesture cost me nothing.

Despite his lifelong efforts my father never made a man of me, certainly not the man he envisioned. I had neither the inclination nor the desire for that. He did succeed in making me think about what it means to be a man. I finally came to believe that men are made from the sum of their experiences; and the quality of the man is not determined by the experiences themselves, but by what he makes of them.

I am now a man of fifty-six at the end of my first year in Palm Springs. I do not miss San Francisco because I enjoy the postcards of memory she has left behind. I review them occasionally in quiet moments of solitude or surrender to their guidance on nocturnal flights of fantasy that once again give voices to the dead.

When I return to San Francisco in person, I find myself growing more anxious each day to put the cool, gray city of love behind me and return to the warmth and serenity of the desert. San Franciscans are justifiably chauvinistic about their city, her beauty and desirability. They are also myopic, resistant to change, and seemingly unaware that the once embracing social climate of San Francisco has morphed into a hotbed of N.I.M.B.Y. activism and petty political posturing.

Many gay men and women of my generation are abandoning San Francisco and turning to the desert to reimagine themselves and their environment. For the last decade we have been transforming life in Palm Springs one house, one business, one resort at a time, reinventing a small town essentially abandoned by the movie stars and founding heterosexual families who first discovered and promoted its charms.

The change in Palm Springs recalls the transformation of San Francisco's Castro District which was a working-class Irish neighborhood when I first lived there in 1974, and where homes now start at $1 million. Like San Francisco, no candidate for political office in Palm Springs can now be elected without the gay vote. The significance of this change is startling when you understand that Palm Springs in the 1980s had no gay bars or clubs because politicians and city officials conspired to keep them outside the city limits.

The gay population of Palm Springs is a graying gay population, but we will not age like our parents. We will probably not take up golf and quilting is out of the question. And although we remain as susceptible to boomer egocentrism as our heterosexual peers, our journey is distinctly different from theirs.

The 1969 Stonewall rebellion in New York was the watershed moment for my gay generation. The generation before us pretended to be something they were not in order to survive, or they remained at home and became the dutiful caretaker of an aging parent. We would not make these choices. But our individual and collective decision to live an openly gay life as soon as we reached adulthood in the late sixties and early seventies came with unique challenges. We did not marry and have children and live the socially acceptable lie. We did not for a moment pretend to be something we were not, and this makes us different. Pushing ourselves away from the starting line we raced toward a new urban gay identity, one completely different from that of the closeted gay men and women who preceded us. We had no guidebook to follow, no precedent for the way we would define ourselves, and no road map to show how we could reshape popular culture to accommodate our presence. We would sometimes be forced to sacrifice social acceptance, professional standing, and financial security in order to pioneer a new way of being.

In the middle of our lives, when we were making progress on all fronts, we were hit with a plague that devastated our numbers. We were not felled by our sexual orientation or by sex, but by a virus. A generation was lost and, after all the progress of the 1970s, we had to continue fighting for equality and self-determination while burying our own. And there can be no doubt about this: in the early years of the health crisis we cared for each other because no one outside our community would. AIDS was first given the scientifically preposterous label "gay-related immuno-deficiency." We became social pariahs.

Given the challenges, it should come as no surprise when, in the face of old age we make bad fashion choices, behave self-indulgently, become sexually fixated, have bad hair days, and sometimes wax Peter Pan-ish. There was no archetype for the mature, successful, openly gay person. This creature simply did not exist in our society. Even now I don't know a single gay man older than myself who embodies all the spiritual, intellectual, emotional, and physical qualities I would like to emulate or use as a template for aging. I would love to have someone like this to turn to because I haven't the slightest idea how to grow old. In this respect, I am clueless. While still in my thirties I became convinced old age was not within the realm of the possible for me. Like most gay men of my generation I continue to make it up as I go along. As survivors, we now remain reluctant pioneers on a frontier whose borders must expand to encompass aging.

But I did not move to Palm Springs to die or retire. I came to reinvent myself one more time, knowing I am not the person I once was. My needs, tastes, and desires have changed. I now elect to live in a small town on the edge of a California desert where people are nice and the cost of living is almost affordable. I listen to oldies stations; I do not know how to download music onto my own iPod; I have never played a video game; I could not identify an X-Box if you placed one in front of me; and I am less likely to send a text message than Jewel is to get orthodontia. I am willing to gladly surrender the things of youth, but what will I replace them with? I don't have an answer for that question. So I go about each day examining opportunities as they present themselves and trying them on for size. I have yet to find a comfortable fit.

A life unfolds like a motion picture, one in which we each serve as our own screenwriter, star, and director. In her memoir, *You'll Never Eat Lunch in This Town Again*, the late film producer Julia Phillips revealed her personal cinematic mantra. Whenever she wanted to extract herself from a difficult situation or absolve herself from personal responsibility, Phillips was fond of saying, "This is not my movie." I am drawn to a more affirmative statement.

This is my movie. I am now prepping my lines and assembling the supporting players for a new location shoot. The screenplay is incomplete and the reviews may be unfavorable, but I'm comfortable knowing there will be only one name in the credits. Background, reset to one.

Printed in the United States
95463LV00006B/113/A

9 781430 322849